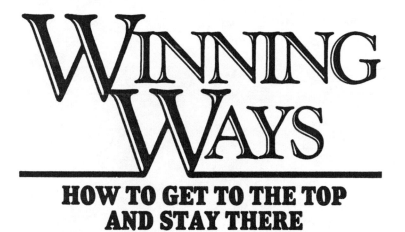

WINNING WAYS

HOW TO GET TO THE TOP
AND STAY THERE

ISBN 0-9621370-0-6

ii

WINNING WAYS

HOW TO GET TO THE TOP AND STAY THERE

By Dr. Gayle Carson

EDITED BY CHARLES FLOWERS

Cover design by Rose DeFabio
Cover photograph by Dan Littlejohn

About the author:

GAYLE CARSON is a popular lecturer to corporations and business groups. An entrepreneur all of her adult life, she bought her own business at the age of 21, and later was named Florida's Outstanding Young Woman of America. She was the first woman to chair the South Florida Better Business Bureau, and lives in Miami Beach. She holds a doctorate in education from Nova University.

About the editor:

CHARLES FLOWERS is an award-winning writer for many national newspapers and magazines including *Newsweek, The New York Times,* and *The Washington Post,* and has edited other books on business and parenting. He lives in Fort Lauderdale, Florida.

Contents

Foreword

"What do I need to do to become a successful speaker?" was a question asked of me by a brand new member at a recent meeting of the National Speakers Association. "Have something to say to other people and *earn the right to say it*" was my response. Regrettably, there are many people who are still looking for the "magic pill" that will produce instant success, whether that be as a speaker, a salesperson, an engineer, or a manager. I know many successful people, but I don't know a single one who hasn't paid his or her "dues" in order to achieve that success. There are hundreds of so-called "self-help" books that purport to offer the latest version of "Ten Easy Steps to Success." This book is NOT one of those.

No one knows better than Gayle Carson that the road to success is long and filled with ditches and detours. Furthermore, that road is a continuous journey, never a destination. This book can help you, the reader, come to grips with the answers to three fundamental questions:

What does real success mean for me?
Am I willing to pay the price to achieve that success?

(If the answer is "yes") **What do I really need to get there?**

If you decide to proceed on this journey, this book will be an invaluable road map. It may cause you to periodically assess, and even modify, your definition of success. It may lead you to wonder at times if the journey is worth the effort. As you achieve some of the milestones described here, you will feel a sense of empowerment and exhiliration that is far more fulfilling and long lasting than any chemically-induced experience. It is the ultimate "high."

Get ready for an arduous, but exciting, trip to real self-fulfillment.

—*George L. Morrisey, CPAE*

(Editor's note: George L. Morrisey is the author of 14 books, including **Getting Your Act Together: Goal Setting For Fun, Health and Profit,** *and* **The Executive Guide to Strategic Planning.** *He was recognized in 1984 with the CPAE (Council of Peers Award for Excellence) the highest recognition granted to a professional speaker. Others selected to this award include Art Linkletter, Og Mandino, Norman Vincent Peale, and Zig Ziglar. Mr. Morrisey is chairman of The Morrisey Group, a management consulting firm based in Buena Park, California.)*

Acknowledgements

To my editor, Charles Flowers, I express my deepfelt thanks, for his time, energy, guidance and support. To my husband, Norm, I give my love; to my children Scott, Tracy and Steve, my support and understanding, and to my mother and father, I give thanks for their guidance, wisdom and value over the many years.

Also by Gayle Carson...

Videotapes on every aspect of professional development, including:

Creating a Winning Image

Goal-Setting and Priority Planning

Is Selling a Numbers Game?

Tools of the Professional

And audiotapes to help you grow while you listen:

Coaching, Counseling and Motivating Employees

Creating a Winning Image — for Women Only

Let's Talk Business:
Telephone Skills & Customer Relations

Making Time Work for You

The Leading Edge:
Assertive Management and Stress Control

Gayle is also featured in "Star-Spangled Speakers," which is full of information from top professional speakers who tell how they "made it."

For price and ordering information, call or write:

Gayle N. Carson
2957 Flamingo Drive
Miami Beach, FL 33140-3916
(305) 534-8846

Introduction

When Gayle Carson asked me to help put together her first book, I had a mixture of pleasure, doubt, and fear. The doubt came from the feeling that we might not have anything new to say on the subject of success. The fear came from the same nagging place it always does, that nothing we ever do is enough. The pleasure came to dominate the other emotions as I got to know a woman who is as tough as she is bright, and who truly does have a message worth sharing.

We surveyed the "success" literature before concluding that there was something basically missing that Gayle had been providing to her corporate clients for years: simple, direct, personal changes that can lead to individual and business success. How one dresses, speaks or doesn't speak, listens or fails to listen, sets goals, negotiates, and leads may not have everything to do with success. But it has a lot to do with it. It is my belief that anyone can profit from the insights she makes in these areas. Women, especially, who rightly see Gayle Carson as a positive role model can take her ideas to heart. Men can also learn from her, as I am evidence.

This book is organized in five sections: The Winning Formula, The Winning Image, Winning Communications, The Winning Way To the Top and Winning Converts. In plain language, Gayle tells you how you can improve in each of these areas, and how all of them are necessary to your success. Her chapters on telephone skills, public speaking and the "A's, B's, C's and D's of Personality" are worth the price of admission alone.

Our collaboration has been beneficial to me because it has put me in contact with a woman who does not know the meaning of the word "quit." In her life, as in her business, Gayle practices what she preaches. But this is not a sermon. It's a practical way up, a method—if you apply it with persistence and discipline—to go as high as you dare to dream.

—*Charles Flowers*
Fort Lauderdale, Florida
July, 1988

Part I: *The Winning Formula*

CHAPTER 1
Success Equals Persistence Plus Discipline

"People often ask me if I know the secret of success, and if I could tell others how to make their dreams come true. My answer is: you do it by working."

—Walt Disney

There is always somebody who tries harder. Do you believe that statement? If you do, you may be in the wrong book. Because no other ingredient is more important to your success than effort. There is always someone stronger, faster, smarter and better looking. That's a statistical certainty unless you happen to be Superman or Wonder Woman. But no one needs to be more persistent.

Persistence is defined by the situation. You are foolish, not persistent, if you are a professional gambler who sorts through his losing tickets and kicks himself for the way he bet. Or, to extend the metaphor only slightly, if you are a professional stockbroker who does the same thing. You learn from your mistakes, you don't wallow in them.

You are foolish, not persistent, if you repeat the same process in the same way over and over again even though you know it hasn't worked yet and the only thing keeping you from trying something new is fear of the new. You are foolish, not persistent, if you ignore the lessons of the environment and the wise teachers who have been placed on earth to help you succeed.

But, you are persistent, not foolish, if you conscientiously pursue a hard-to-sell client or job prospect, if you show yourself to be capable in ways that can't escape the attention of your prospect, your boss or others who are significant to your career. Your persistence will win admirers if you chart a course for yourself and refuse to deviate from it.

You are persistent, not foolish, if you analyze yourself from your client's point of view: Why do I need him or her? What about them makes me want to do business with them? What unique qualities, knowledge or skills do they have? And when you begin to listen honestly, those answers will start coming in the affirmative, and you will have the tools you need to go beyond the place where you are now to the place you want to be. Your persistence will give you the answers you need to make critical changes in the way you are perceived, which is crucial to success in almost any field of human endeavor. Your persistence as well as other skills you can develop, will help you to recognize your mistakes and learn from them. You can even use persistence to dodge the traps you may have used to keep yourself from succeeding. If you don't quit, you can't be beaten. It's that simple.

Discipline is also crucial. Discipline is the learned ability to do the same thing over and over and over again. It requires discipline to perform tasks you don't like. Discipline is that ability to form a pattern, to establish a methodology of making yourself more responsible for yourself, and the best framework from within which you build.

In this book we shall learn of successful men and women who applied this basic formula. We shall explore many of the fine points of image and career strategy, effective communication and leadership. But without persistence and discipline—plotting a course and sticking to it—no amount of image-building or imagination will get you there.

I firmly believe that you can accomplish anything you put your mind to regardless of your financial status, professional education or family background, providing you have the basic talent and abilities required, keep an open mind and lay a plan for yourself. The two most important ingredients in your plan should be persistence and discipline. You must pursue your goal relentlessly and never get sidetracked. Nothing can interfere with your thought processes. Third, you must appreciate yourself and your accomplishments. If you don't understand how to handle success, it will handle you. You need to learn to take from it to get to the next step, and to give back to it through the community, your co-workers or employees, and the people who share your life. If you don't, there will be an empty void that will not make anything you have worthwhile.

You must also face up to what you have to contribute and sacrifice to be successful. If study, either by formal education, seminars, reading or training programs, is necessary, don't make excuses as to why you don't have the time or money to pursue them. Find a way. If you are asked to take an active part in a professional organization or trade association, do so. You'll find the credits far outbalance any debits. People in your profession will get to know who you are, your abilities and your strengths. That is important for your profession, credibility and visibility. Try to get as much publicity and coverage for your ideas and creativity as possible. Develop an aura of business, cleverness and importance about the things you do. And when the chips are down, know your stuff and be able to come through.

Concentrate On Getting There

The only limits you will experience are those you place on yourself. You must be prepared to give up your social life, much of your family life and concentrate on all the goodies of "getting there." But if you allow time for a good physical fitness plan so that the hours you work and the stress you experience will be tolerable, you will find you will be able to function quite well. You should also learn how to make the social life you do have leisurely, so that you can relax and enjoy it more easily, although you will probably find many of the social events you attend are semi-business as well. Since family time will be short, you should be sure it is quality time.

But you should realize one important thing: the first ten years in business are your formative ones, the learning times that can never be replaced. Your enthusiasm and determination will never be higher. They ARE important years and part of the "dues paying" era. The lessons you learn when applied will allow you to work smart instead of working hard later on.

A Personal Aside

I never knew I could fail, therefore there was nothing preventing me from succeeding. I never fully understood this until just a few years ago when my sister said to me, "Gayle, we were programmed to achieve from the day we were born." Although I had never really thought much about it, I was raised very independently and taught to take care of myself at an early age. I also was forced to face unpleasant situations head-on and deal with them in the present instead of delaying them for some later time. I was always taught right from wrong, and the need for responsibility and ethics. If there was a problem with a friend, I had to confront it. If a second boy asked me for a date and I had already turned the first one down, I couldn't go. If I didn't understand something, I was told to investigate. Mainly, I was shown that I couldn't hide, and that life was not always fair, but that if you did learn how to handle things, you would survive.

I clearly remember at the age of eight having to phone in the drug orders of my pharmacist father to the supply house, verbalizing names I couldn't even pronounce. My mother told me then that someday I would need to know how to talk on the phone. For nearly thirty years my businesses have been built over the telephone and I feel as at home with the phone as I do my own family. Partly from that experience, I have come to love the phone. Every time it rings, I get excited. I never know who will be on the other end, and it is usually good news. I can't even imagine going somewhere where there is no phone, and I try and bring that attitude to people who call me.

At the age of twenty, after graduating from college, I moved to Miami with two suitcases and a lot of hope to try and make it in just two weeks. I was determined to have my own modeling school, but knew I had to learn the territory and the business end of things. I trekked from school to school and finally found the exact one at which I wanted to work. It was small and personal—the kind of place that seemed real, and didn't offer customers the moon. It seemed more like family than a strange new job. At first I was offered part-time employment, but after two weeks I was given a position as the owner's assistant. She fired the girl who had been with her for two and a half years because as she said, "Gayle, you're going to make money for somebody and it might as well be me."

For the first two weeks I was in the office and never saw my employer. I got an education in a hurry. I used my instinct and common sense. If someone asked me a question and I didn't have the answer, I figured out that I needed to get it somewhere, and what better place than the owner? My yellow pad was filled with questions at the end of the day—it was quite a way to get started, but it gave me what I needed in a short period of time. Within a month, I had the swing of things, within four months I had tripled my salary (which was practically nothing to begin with) and within eight months I had bought the business. At twenty-one I owned a business (all on borrowed money, of course), had monthly notes to meet, employees to deal with and was wondering what I had to do to get customers to call and clients to walk through the door.

In the beginning, there were days that could not be filled. I had free time on my hands and moments when the checkbook never seemed to stretch until the end of the week. At first I felt sorry for myself, but then I decided there was only one way to get the business, and that was to go out and find it. I began to join business clubs and trade associations and became an active participant. I gave free lectures at every civic and community organization I could find and began going to local high schools one day a week. Little by little my business began to grow and soon there were no more free days. I found that between the lectures, teaching and agency work, four days turned into seven, and the twelve-hour day was the norm rather than the exception. But I loved every minute of it, and all other activities, including my social life, took a back seat to my business.

Finding a Mentor

After three years, everything was paid off, I had money in the bank, my credit was built up and within the next year I would marry and open my second school. This operation moved four times within the next four years, each time to larger quarters. I had a marvelous teacher-manager who stayed with me twenty years as a model and tour hostess. I believe mentoring is important, but not necessarily in the formal sense of superior to employee or great one above to lowly person below. If we're smart, we are always going through a mentoring process, learning from those whom circumstances place in front of us, taking from their knowledge and experience whatever they care to give us. Our task is to decide what it is we want to know—and find the best person to impart that knowledge to us. Usually, whether it's the mechanic you ask for an opinion about a car, or a television executive you ask for a good place to study broadcasting, they are most happy to be consulted. You cannot overlook good information when changing cars—or careers.

My next endeavor was a real estate school. Since my husband was a builder and we both had an avid interest in real estate investments, it seemed the most natural path to follow. I already had a broker's license and new laws were being passed that tightly controlled vocational and technical schools. I felt that if I had to do all the paperwork involved for modeling schools, I might as well expand to more difficult and potentially profitable fields. I was fortunate that one of the nationwide real estate firms showed an interest in my school and provided me with interested students.

This eventually took me into a sixth school which incorporated areas of travel, fashion merchandising, court reporting and training legal and medical secretaries. At this point, I had several people working for me, but there was still a never-ending amount of detail to attend to. This was my way of life, however, and everything had been built around it . . . my marriage, my children, my leisure activities.

No one else could understand how I could possibly like the merry-go-round I was on. By this time, I was lecturing two to three days a week in the high schools. That meant getting up at six a.m. and lecturing from seven a.m. to two p.m. From there I would go into one of the schools and work until nine-thirty primarily on sales, interviews and record-keeping. There were also organizational and staff meetings, other civic lectures, agency supervision and general day-to-day activities. Everyone in my house cooperated and I am positive my youngest son was twelve before he realized all mothers didn't work. After all, I had been working the day he was born and was back to work two weeks later. Even my marriage was on Thanksgiving eve, because Thanksgiving was the only day I could take off. I have been one of the most fortunate people in the world to have found a husband who, although in a completely different profession, has never stopped me from building a separate, successful career.

There were compensations. In 1970, I had been named Florida's Outstanding Young Woman of America; in 1973–75 I was elected International President of the Modeling Association of America, and the school was selected as "School of the Year" by the Modeling Association of America, International. But best of all, I absolutely loved every minute of my life. So why change? There is only one answer: Because it was time.

Changing Course: A Sense of Timing

I knew I had developed the business to its maximum under my tutelage. It had made me a strong person with guts and determination, fair but not easily stepped upon. My name was well-known in the community and I had kept my own name after marriage before it was fashionable. It was as if I was two distinctly different people. I had now spent the last twenty-one years totally immersed in business. My agency had grown into one that placed talent on national TV commercials as well as in movies. I placed models in photography ads that were seen in national publications and trained promotional models who were never more popular. An opportunity came along to sell the whole package. I had resisted all the overtures in the past. Why was I even considering it? I guess I was ready for more expansion but knew I couldn't do it on my own and I knew from experience that I didn't like partners.

And so I sold and retained a management contract. Life had never been lazier, more boring or frustrating. This was not going to work! I suppose the new owners saw a little girl with six offices, well-known and respected, and thought if I had done this all by myself what could possibly be accomplished with their money and resources. Then, of course, they proceeded to change everything I had done and wanted me "at the desk" eight hours a day.

Step Up To The Podium

For twenty-one years I had been speaking on a regular basis as part of the school and agency promotion. I was also making a tidy second income from convention programs for spouses. During the year as a management executive, I increased my professional speaking and within one month of leaving the operation discovered the National Speakers Association. At my first convention I was completely amazed at all the speakers who were actually making a full-time living at something I thought was absolutely the most fun thing to do in the world.

Originally I had been trained to speak and perform. I was graduated from Emerson College in Boston with a degree in drama, broadcasting and speech. Now I found myself drawn back into performing. From a fifteen-minute panel participation I had done, I was given a contract to become a national television spokesperson for Clairol, and did many local talk show programs. Since I had begun a doctoral program four years earlier, my level of topics had expanded greatly. I found myself in demand as a seminar leader in the university system and as a keynote speaker on time management, decisiveness and priority planning.

Although many arduous hours went into research, format, contacts and promotion, I had finally found the work I wanted to do for the next twenty-one years. I loved speaking—the audiences, the vibrations, the empathy, the feeling that once again I was imparting knowledge. It seemed so natural to me I couldn't believe speaking was number one on the public's list of fears. Speaking in front of a group is as easy for me as building a table is for my husband. Of course I get nervous, I question my material, the methods by which I reach my audience, but the bottom line is . . . I love it.

One of the reasons I feel it is fairly easy to be successful, if you have a career path to follow, is the fact that there are so many losers walking around feeling sorry for themselves and destroying their minds with drugs, alcohol and neuroses. While they are talking about how everyone is against them, and making excuses for all their failures, other people are slowly plodding along and eventually "making it."

Persist!

An average person who applies himself will be able to rise to the greatest heights if he only tries over and over again. Most of our great achievers got where they are only after many frustrations and disappointments. You never hear about the rough times, however, because people usually don't want to acknowledge them. Ronald Reagan is a good example. How many people know he is the son of an alcoholic who had a hard time growing up during the Depression? It certainly isn't a point he brings up, but surmounting those difficulties helped him mature, and may have taught him other valuable lessons as well. Eleanor Roosevelt and Betty Ford were reared in similar circumstances.

I wish each of you the happiness of great achievement in whatever you choose to do, but I also encourage you to plan your life and lifestyle so that it is positive for you and not harmful to others. If you have a plan to follow, you should have no problem getting to where you want to go. Learn to discipline yourself so that whenever you get sidetracked, you always have something to go back to, to keep yourself on target. But your plan should never compromise your ethical and moral values, nor hurt anyone else. Your life will be enriched if you have the compassion to understand and aid your friends, co-workers and family when you least need to do so. Although not always fashionable, the truly good person who is an achiever is a doer and a fine human being whose success does not subtract from the world, but makes it a better place. All it takes is believing in yourself, and the courage to take a chance.

By reading this book, you have taken a small chance in the hope of improving your life. Perhaps you are hoping for one small thing that you can learn, and apply to bring you immediate riches. Good luck finding it. More likely is the possibility that several areas will need improving, honing and sharpening. And even the areas in which you are strongest will need refreshment if you are to achieve beyond your current level. I hope you find that single nugget, if that's all you seek. But I have a stronger hope, and wish for each of you: That this book begins to outline the territory for your personal and lifelong exploration.

CHAPTER 2
Success Ethics: What Will You Do To Get What You Want?

"The moral flabbiness born of the exclusive worship of the bitch-goddess success. That—with the squalid cash interpretation put on the word success—is our national disease."
—William James in a 1906 letter to H.G. Wells

In this country, we often talk of ethic and ethics, singular and plural. There is the so-called work ethic, the Protestant ethic, and the ethic of social responsibility. Ethics, whether held in common with a group or individually as one who marches to a different drummer, are basic principles of right or good conduct. And whether one shares the ethics or the customs of one's business associates, or not, it is important to know what they are. Different customs are prevalent in different regions of the country, among differing faiths, and even within different businesses.

For example, the moral value placed on objectivity in journalism is almost unknown outside of the United States, and even within this country there are strong variants from *The New York Times* ("All the news that's fit to print.") to the *National Enquirer* ("Inquiring minds want to know.") Interestingly, many of the newspapers which seem biased on their face are owned by foreign-trained publishers who bought American properties, and adapted them in ways they had seen succeed elsewhere. And as the circulation of publications like the *Enquirer* demonstrate, they were right.

Success itself, then, is no measure of morality. Yet, one can seek monetary success with a clear conscience, if no ethical shortcuts are taken. To help sort this thorny subject out, and overcome the roadblocks to your success, we shall explore in this chapter the meanings of success and ethics.

Humility Revisited: Do Nice Guys Finish Last?

Tradition holds that humility is a quality to be nurtured, that work itself is good. And these ethics, combined with those institutionalized in our government (freedom, self-determination, etc.) have combined to create the basic fabric by which Americans do business. We respect honesty, integrity, and humility because those ethics are so well woven thoughout our common human history.

In our century, which has seen the creation of a huge middle class, success has carried at least a hint of disrepute, of vanity. We heard from William James, the successful novelist, about his "bitch-goddess." Other 20th Century contributions to the definition of success include philosopher Bertrand Russell, who in his 1930 book *The Conquest of Happiness* said, "Unless a man has been taught what to do with success after getting it, the achievement of it must inevitably lead to boredom." Classic film actress Liv Ullmann echoed that sentiment: "The best thing that comes with success is the knowledge that it is nothing to long for." The poet T.S. Eliot put it more cleverly in his play *The Family Reunion*: "Success is relative. It is what we can make of the mess we have made of things." A few of the popular opinions that diverge from these were former baseball manager Leo Durocher: "Nice guys finish last." And "Playboy philospher" Hugh Hefner: "I've been poor and I've been rich, and rich is better."

Actually, the notion of success has been scorned throughout history by those who, had they not achieved it in their lives and work, may have felt altogether differently. Oliver Wendell Holmes, a beloved Chief Justice of the U.S. Supreme Court, reflected at age 90: "There is only one success—to be able to spend your own life in your own way."

Questions of Conscience: What Will You Do?

I believe you can get to where you want to go without cheating, stealing or hurting someone else. I also believe there are times when you will have to compromise. Each compromise becomes a value choice. For instance, when you really have a strong opinion on something and believe in it deeply—but you know your boss feels the opposite way—how hard do you push? If you catch someone in a lie, but you know they will be hurt and embarrassed when you confront them with it, do you turn the other cheek? When you know someone has sniped you in the back, but they come on to you in a warm and friendly manner, do you smile in return, or plot revenge?

The questions are endlesss, and there are no easy answers. Each person must solve them according to his or her own "success ethics."

If you are a stickler for quality, how do you feel about working for a firm that fudges on quality standards in order to improve the "bottom line?" Or for a boss who pads expense accounts, or for a system that is cool to suggestions from employees? Does your company practice "forced retirement" under any name? If you are a woman in middle management, how do you feel when the idea you suggested fifteen minutes ago, and were ignored, surfaces again from the mouth of some man and is met with approval. Do you laugh about it, or cry?

Whatever decision you reach, the most important thing is that it is *your* decision, and that you arrive at it after studying what is best for you, and where you are on your career ladder and your life ladder. Responsibilities to a spouse and children may color your perspective one day, while ten years down the road you may have a totally different view.

The most important credo is to be true to yourself. If you don't believe in the reasons why you are working where you are, you will be a lonely, dissatisfied and unhappy person. Lawrence Mizner once said, "Be careful how you treat people on the way up, because you might pass them on the way down." You should never be too busy to share, give sincere advice, respond to someone in need or give of yourself. You don't always have to make time right then and there, but you should make some time

15

at some point. The friends and partners you will create will help you in return. What goes around does come around.

Sometimes when you are at the top and enjoying all the trappings of success, you begin to believe your own press clippings. You may start to think that you are the only one with the knowledge and the answers. You stop paying attention to the "little people," the people whose loyalty and efficiency got you where you are. You may stop caring as you start to believe there is "not enough time" or need to "sweat the small stuff." This can be fatal arrogance, not to mention a cause of loneliness and bitterness. Remember there is always someone waiting to take your place and some bright, young, clever entrepreneur who has the ideas, guts and enthusiasm to come up with a better mousetrap.

Game-playing: A Necessary Evil

A lot of games go on in the corporate world. Not only is it important to recognize that games are going on, in order to find an appropriate position for yourself before the final gun goes off, but it certainly helps to know the rules. These are not usually found in a company handbook, but rather in the values, mission, philosophy and goals of your employer. Once you figure out the essentials (and these are more often than not unwritten rules), ask yourself these key questions:

—Do I subscribe to these rules?
—If I don't, can I hold my tongue?
—Do I fit into the mold?
—If I don't now, can I compromise?
—Can I work with someone I don't respect?
—What if things are fine here, but disastrous nearby?

Can you work in an atmosphere of camaraderie, spirit and accomplishment, while every other department is disorganized and uncooperative? In short, can you make the decision to change it or live with it? (For help with these fundamental questions, see the next chapter on goal-setting).

Once you have answers to these questions, you know where you stand. The most important ingredient to success is attitude.

Studies show that if your business is serving food, the attitude of the people serving will have more to do with the restaurant's success than either the quality of the food or the price. People will pay more than food is worth, and they will even overlook slightly inferior dishes. But they will *never* come back to a place where they feel they were unfairly treated. Smart, successful restaurateurs and their staffs know this. And if they can stay upbeat in that pressure-packed atmosphere, what's stopping you?

You make out of anything exactly what you want it to be. There are certainly obstacles in many situations, but how you deal with them and what you learn from them are the most important keys to your personal and professional growth. A songwriter once said, "Nothing bad ever happens to me. It's all new material." How you visualize, how you conduct yourself, how you treat others *and yourself* will build for you a reputation and that will do more for your credibility than anything else.

While we're on the subject of games, we know it's not the final score that matters, or how many times we get knocked down. It's how we play our part, and the fact that we get up at least one more time than we get decked.

Commitment to Ideals: Essence of Leadership

Persistence and discipline are two of the crucial factors to any success. But there is one more, and that is commitment. Commitment means more than persistence. Commitment means doing something over and over until you get it right; and it may mean sticking to something when it would be far easier to let go. It means listening to all sides of a story with interest and compassion, but still carrying on with what you think is right. Commitment is a visible promise to yourself and others even when something better might come along. Commitment to ideals earns you points in ways you can see and ways which maybe you can't. It is the essence of leadership.

In their book *Winning Performance*, which analyzed successful midsize companies, Donald Clifford and Richard Cavanagh identified six distinctive characteristics of winning corporate leaders:

1. They instill a strong sense of mission and shared values—constantly to reinforce a deeply ingrained set of beliefs.
2. They pay relentless attention to business fundamentals.
3. They treat bureaucracy as an archenemy.
4. They encourage experimentation.
5. They think like their customers, and work hard on behalf of them. And
6. They count on people and put development and motivation of their people at the top of their list of priorities.

Success is impossible, or at least extremely unlikely, without a shared sense of values, and beliefs. That is why it is important that you learn "success ethics."

Leadership is also critical to success. Without effective leadership, you are an enterprise of one. With leadership, you can marshal an army. Today's leader has to be a visionary, and be charismatic. He or she must command a following and inspire others. Today's leader must be tangible and accessible to employees, or at minimum be seen to be accessible. Good ideas as well as talent come from the bottom of any organization. Do not wall yourself off from those who can help you get where you're going. Every battle needs foot soldiers.

This is not to say there are no differences between a "worker ethic" and a "manager ethic." Someone who prefers to work for an hourly wage will always see things differently from a manager, who must get things done through other people no matter how long it takes. Managers are defined, in large part, by their ability to build a cohesive force in the office. They are judged by superiors who expect certain results. Usually, there is a hidden irony in the differences between workers and managers. While workers may grumble about job conditions or pay, they have usually accepted certain limits on their expectations. Managers, on the other hand, are never truly content with the way things are, least of all their salary or place on the career ladder, because they are on an upwardly mobile career path.

Managers, it should be noted, are not necessarily good leaders, and leaders are not necessarily good managers. It is extremely fortunate if both sets of qualities are found in one person, especially when they have not been developed. But managers tend to be more task-oriented, while leaders are inspirational, motivational and charismatic.

Success Is More Than Money

Ideals and ethics can clash even within two-career families, so why should we be amazed to find lack of uniformity in a corporation? Survival is tough, but to make it worthwhile we need values and ethics.

To some it is money, because that is the most tangible and visible evidence of success. It may be the way you keep score. Success is certainly something that other people use to keep score about you. Success buys concrete, material things which are visible to all. But there are, as we all know, things that money can't buy.

Money is nice, and it is important, if only because the opposite condition is usually unbearable. Not having money means not having the tools we need to live, the fruit to be planted as a seed or enjoyed now. Having money means freedom from worry about bills and the ability to provide the things you want to provide for those who depend on you. Money can buy a lot of peace and security. But we must keep it in perspective. Neither peace nor security is absolute.

Success also includes happiness. Unless you truly love what you do, you will never get where you want to go. You cannot maintain the enthusiasm or the excitement necessary to motivate the people around you if you don't show it yourself. You have to know your stuff, but you also have to believe in it. Because they will be the first to pick up on it if you don't. It is your smile, your manner, your image, your conduct that sets the tone for everyone and everything around you.

Success may mean working for your community. This work could be through a service organization, although it is important not to confuse commerce with social consciousness. Your own hard work can mean a lot to volunteer groups. In this area as in all others, make sure the work matters. You could also make charitable contributions to causes you feel are worthwhile. Studies show that people on the way up already know this and donate a bigger chunk of their income (about 3 percent) to charities than do others. How you feel about this question may have much to do with the way you see yourself, as a taker or a giver. And the gifts in terms of self-image will come back to you.

Maybe your idea of success is the ability to develop a new method, a new idea, a new way of doing business that has never been done before. Perhaps starting a new career or business or movement is what you have in mind. (For help with that decision, see Chapter 16.)

Whatever definition of sucess you subscribe to, the most important thing is to be good at whatever it is you do. Be the best you can be. Treat people well and emulate always the kind of person you want to be, and the qualities you admire in others. Do these things, and unqualified success will come to you.

CHAPTER 3
Set Unrealistic Goals with Realistic Timetables

"If you want to succeed, you should strike out on new paths rather than travel the worn paths of accepted success."
—John D. Rockefeller, Sr.

Success is not an easy road. Yet, for many who have succeeded in a variety of endeavors, the path, though prickly and different from any they had known, was almost irresistible. Some say the ability to take risks divides the successful from the also-rans. I say it another way: It's the ability to *set unrealistic goals with realistic timetables* that creates the *possibility* for success.

Face it, how realistic was it for Maurice Mickelwhite, whose family had worked for the Billingsgate Fish Market in England for more than 300 years, to formulate the desire to become an actor? When he began to work on the stage, family and friends would ask him, "Who do you think you are?" He knew who he was not: Maurice Mickelwhite, fish peddler. He became Michael Caine, one of the most successful actors of his generation, Oscar-winning performer and the heir apparent to the legacy of another popular male actor, the late Cary Grant, who began *his* Academy Award-winning career as a Coney Island lifeguard. Caine summed up his life choice in words every unrealistic goal-setter can appreciate, in an interview with Ed Bradley on *60 Minutes*: "I decided not to back off." The movies, perhaps more publicly than any medium, serves up a diet of "success stories" like these—people who did not wait to be discovered, but who instead got themselves unstuck from dead-end, predictable futures.

Writers know rejection, too. William Kennedy won the Pulitzer Prize for fiction in 1984 for his novel *Ironweed*. Thirteen different publishers rejected it before the Pulitzer committee decided it was one of America's best. A movie offer soon followed.

The sports world is even more replete with men and women who, by example, taught the rest of us that we need not be bound by the restrictions of the past. The past can hold us in its grip in two ways. Our individual pasts can give us scripts which order our behavior, narrowly define our talents and expand our shortcomings. And our collective past histories create restrictive social rules. Sometimes, to be successful, you have to break a few rules, shake a few people up, change the social order. Jackie Robinson, who broke Major League Baseball's color line in 1948 when he played for the Brooklyn Dodgers, did all of that and more. Robinson may have drawn a breath of inspiration from Jim Thorpe, an Oklahoma reservation-born Indian who rose to become an Olympic decathlon champion, and competed in professional football and baseball. Billie Jean King and Ann Meyer set new standards for women's tennis and basketball, by competing successfully against men.

But for sheer miracle of achievement, none of these sports heroes compares with Jeff Blatnick, the wrestler who won a gold medal in his class in the 1984 Olympics after being told he had incurable Hodgkin's disease and could never compete again. Who can forget the words Blatnick spoke through tear-streaked eyes as he came off the mat in Los Angeles in triumph: "I'm a happy dude!"

Happiness through self-actualization is one of the real attractions for winners; not wealth. Happiness does not just happen to you, it comes through your actions and perception and timing. Happiness is the realization of one's potential, often despite heavy odds, which makes it all the sweeter. To achieve success in spite of those odds requires the setting of unrealistic goals. Being overly realistic can be the kiss of death to your dreams.

Be Realistic About Time

The place to be realistic is in your timetable for achieving those goals. Obviously, if you plan to compete in an arena where the race does go to the swiftest, it is a good idea to start early. Such endeavors as sports (especially such teen-dominated ones as swimming and tennis), and beauty pageants readily come to mind. If you want to be Miss America or to oust Martina Navratilova in straight sets at Wimbledon, it would be a good idea to check your progress at about age 15. And even if your goals are a little more down to earth, steady and regular checking and re-definition is always a good idea.

What are the limits imposed by "reality," anyway? There are certain physical limitations, but those have been broken in sports and entertainment and virtually every other field. You don't have to be any given height to succeed, or weight, or be born one favored sex or race or religion to make it. The limitations are all upstairs, in that Catch-22 known as self-esteem. As our own worst critics, we value ourselves because of our successes. But we achieve success often because we have the confidence to risk failure.

To get over limitations is the object lesson here; not to deny their existence. To see what obstacles to success may have been placed in your path, and by whom, ask yourself the following questions:

—How successful have you been in the past and how many times have you been shot down?

—Who usually did the shooting? Was it verbal, in the form of a denial of your ability to do the thing at issue? Can you remember the exact language?

—Does the failure still hurt? Can the painful memory be used to motivate you beyond that first failure? Can you get past this stumbling block or does the brass ring always seem a little bit out of your grasp?

—Can you, knowing all this, think big enough, unrealistic enough to try for something better? Can you summon all of those real and imaginary doubters, and tell them flat out, "Yes, I can!"

How to Set Goals

Timing is a critical part of any success story. And the goals which you write down are the script for yours. I insist that goal-setting works infinitely better when the goals are written down. Not only is there a ready checklist of your objectives and priorities, but the very act of writing them forces you to take control and get organized. If you are to chart a course for yourself, you must have an idea of where you want to go! Written lists of goals do that. More basically, they help you to order and control your day.

Once you control how and where your day goes, the weeks and months will fall into place. By setting daily goals and objectives, you will learn to give priority to the activities that provide the benefits, friendships, rewards, comfort and progress you want.

We all must learn to concentrate not just on activities, being busy for its own sake, but also on the results of that activity. Decide on the path you want to follow. Visualize it. Avoid being sidetracked into useless and sometimes troubling activities. Take charge. Write down your own goals with the following criteria in mind:

1. *Goals must be specific and measurable.*
2. *They must be your own personal goals.*
3. *They must be stated positively and in the present. (No, "I will not's"; plenty of "I am's").*
4. *They must be attainable.*
5. *They must aim at basic personality changes.*
6. *They must start with "I".*
7. *They should be fun.*

Keep your goals in a small notebook which you carry with you at all times, and add "a-ha's" to it as you think of them. Haven't you had a brilliant brainstorm in the middle of the night and by the time the morning came, you had forgotten the idea that you were sure was going to change the world? Unfortunately, our minds only allow us to remember, on average, 40 percent of what we want to when we want to, so write it down.

Keep the notebook in sections according to ideas. Your ideas, properly implemented, are what will make or break your success script. Make room for them. As they accumulate, having the ideas organized by section will make it easier for you to find them. Also write your daily "to do" list in this notebook.

Questions for Goal-Setters

Ask yourself these questions in order to refine and distill your goals from the general to the specific. The answers may help you to separate in your mind the goals you think you're *supposed* to have from those which belong to you, which you own:

1. What are my skills and abilities? Usually, we find it easier and more fun to do things that we enjoy. Don't hesitate to visualize abilities which you have developed in a role you consider a "hobby" for possible career goals.

2. Which skills do I most enjoy? Sort out your skills, and research which jobs and professions can be targeted from them. You can then seek interviews with people in these positions and industries, and begin to weigh the pros and cons.

3. What is important in my life? Certainly your goals will change many times. But you need a starting point. Don't let anyone push you into anything you don't really want. Listen to all counsel, then evaluate and decide for yourself.

4. What do I want to be and what does it take? Pehaps it will take time, energy, education and financial support to realize your goals. The only way you can begin is through the careful outline of a workable plan. Learn to divide this plan into bite-size, digestible pieces.

5. What are the major obstacles or roadblocks? Are they inside or outside? Remember, it is far easier to change yourself than to change the rest of the world. Just remember to be realistic about the time you give yourself for the changes.

Surround Yourself With People Who Share Your Goals

The only way to make your goals happen is to surround yourself with people and environments that support your dream. Not every climate supports every plant. Some need more sun, or water. As we mature into careers, distinctions between people also become more apparent, and you need to find the best people to help you grow in the ways you must if you are to reach your goals.

How do you find such people? If you are sincere and hard-working, it will be noticed. And amazing things will occur! You will begin to get noticed, listened to, recommended. And most important, you gain in self-image and self-esteem. You will be empowered.

Volunteer, show up and perform. You will be recognized for what you are: someone on the way up; a winner. To achieve often means trying a little harder. A winner acts to ensure success. A winner takes action.

Visualize for Results

Close your eyes and try to form a mental image of yourself. Visualize who and what you want to be. Use your imagination. Contrary to what some of our teachers told us, dreaming is not wasted time—it nurtures a constructive plan in place of inactivity. Vivid imagination leads to desire which leads to action and belief.

Skeptical? Cut out a picture of what you want or how you want to look. Teenagers do this all the time, and you know, pretty soon they start looking the part of their heroes and heroines. Paste an article on a subject you admire, a person you would like to emulate, in some conspicuous place. Having their words and their eyes looking over your shoulder all the time may help combat fear and procrastination. Look for three-dimensional mentors, too. You would be amazed at the number of successful people who will give you valuable time and help if you approach them courteously.

If you can't find any mentors handy, visit your local library. Seek positive role models. Read biographies of people you admire. In politics, John F. Kennedy's *Profiles in Courage* is still a classic, while in sports virtually any athlete or coach who's had a winning season has a "biography." Be selective. Most of the real winners had to make choices, and so will you. Don't try to be all things to all people. Learn from different areas, but pay your closest attention to fields that really turn you on. You cannot go in too many different directions at once and still get to your goals on time. You must be focused. Listen to positive thinking tapes. And take a hint from the struggles of others to be easy on yourself.

See how many times it took Thomas Edison before he invented the light bulb? It was he who said, "Genius is one percent inspiration and 99 percent perspiration." And how many times did Babe Ruth strike out in the season he hit 60 home runs? And among the gifted, see how being blind affected Louis Braille, who gave all blind persons access to the printed word.

I take heart from fellow speakers Tom Sullivan and Sharon Komlos, both of whom are totally blind yet very much in demand by corporations and shows like *Good Morning America*. Another top-flight speaker, Zig Ziglar, started out selling pots and pans. One of my personal heroes is the late Dorothy Finkelhor, who was a high school dropout before she went back to school to get her Ph.D. She later founded Point Park College in Pittsburgh, and worked as an active professional speaker and "guested" on 250 radio shows in one year.

Plan Ahead for Success

The difference between success and failure is discipline and commitment. Don't over-think or over-analyze—just do it, and track yourself. Look for the circumstances you want in life, and if you can't find them, create them.

Begin by setting goals. Start immediately. Find three things you'd like to accomplish in the next 12 months. You may think a year is a long time, if you now have trouble planning tomorrow. But a year can be a short time when you look back critically and question where the time went and what was accomplished.

You need to consider *now* how to invest the next 365 tomorrows.

CHAPTER 4
Go For It!

"Success. Four flights Thursday morning. All against twenty-one-mile wind. Started from level with engine power alone. Average speed through the air thirty-one miles. Longest fifty-nine seconds. Inform press. Home Christmas."
   —Telegram from Wilbur and Orville Wright to their father, December 17, 1903

There are no completely right or wrong decisions. And not to decide *is* to decide. By forestalling a decision, circumstances often foreclose your options. Making decisions is half the battle. The mere fact that you can use your mind in logical reasoning gives you a tremendous jump on most people.

You cannot look back with regrets, only ahead with learning and experience. Learn from others. Observe them and see what pleases you and what you'd like to change. If you find yourself shaking your head and saying, "There ought to be a better way," find it!

Learn Through Reading

Despite the wonders of the electronic age (this book is being written on a home computer, and it will be typeset on a machine I can barely describe), reading is still the best way to find out how other people live, other systems work, and some of the trials and errors that others have experienced. In reading you meet people you would otherwise never encounter and get insight and motivation from their experiences.

You also increase awareness of language and vocabulary. You learn phrasing and how to get an idea across, how to communicate. There are no barriers to the written word, except the ones you place yourself. Share in the multitude of information available to you. Learn to see through other people's eyes.

Develop a Sense of Humor; Release Your Imagination

Especially, develop a sense of humor. People love to be around others who are pleasant and enjoyable. Don't become a clown, but do keep that smile on your face. It is hard to clench your teeth when you are smiling—and it is hard to be angry when you have a smile.

Don't get in a rut; or if you get in one, don't stay there. Release your imagination. Think about how you can go on to be a well-rounded, interesting person. You can be anything you make up your mind to be and with the right attitude and application of the formula, success = persistence + discipline, you'll be the best you can at it. This doesn't take money and it doesn't require family background—but it does take time, guts, and a willingness to work hard.

Develop a Positive Mental Attitude

Did you know that five minutes of negative thinking takes the body 24 hours to recover from? What a waste of time. Some people actually enjoy walking around with a cloud over their head. What a waste of energy!

Don't allow yourself to be used or abused by these people. Surround yourself with positive thinkers who can share or at least support your goals. You have the choice of saying no to the people who don't ever see the light at the end of the tunnel. The other choice is to stay in there with them. In the long run, your positive mental attitude will take you farther than your negative friends—if it is aided by disciplined goal-setting and review.

Motivation Basics

A man asked me, "How can I motivate employees?" First, you have to find out if the job they're doing is a motivating job. Is what they're doing all day long interesting, exciting? Is it what they really want to do? Is it what they were hired to do? If you had to write a job description, would it be something they really had applied for?

Does the performance matter? Do you let them know that it matters? As Ken Blanchard says in his book, *The One-Minute Manager*, you can limit praise or criticism to a minute and still be effective. If the employee does a good job do you tell them so, or do you just expect it? If you don't *tell* someone they did a good job, resentment builds up and the employee says, "What does it matter? The boss doesn't notice what I do anyway?"

Have the obstacles been removed? Maybe it is some information they need, maybe there's someone else in the office who is a stumbling block, maybe there's a supplier of some sort who needs to give information before you can make a decision. Make sure all obstacles have been removed—that is the key to motivation whether the subject is an employee, or yourself.

You have learned a winning formula in this section: Persistence plus discipline equals success. You have also learned how to test your ethics in order to ensure that the success you seek is worthy of you. And you have learned to be unrealistic in a positive way, by setting goals which at first blush you might think are beyond your ability to achieve. You have learned to be realistic where it counts, in setting timetables for achieving those goals.

The chapters which follow will help show you how to develop a winning image, how to learn effective speech, dress and grooming habits which some people think are trivial, but which are vital to your success. Even more basically, you will learn to manage your mental and physical health, and learn about the critical interplay of these two components of your life.

Once you have prepared for the struggle ahead, we will discuss techniques and strategies for success at various management levels, the winning ways you can use to get to the top and stay there.

Part II: *The Winning Image*

CHAPTER 5
Beyond Health and Fitness: The Winning Image

"We talked to hundreds of executives who weren't successful, and they all told us, 'Oh, I haven't got time to buy my own clothes.' We talked to guys who were at the top; they all had the time."

—John Molloy, author of "Dress For Success"

Whether you are a man or a woman, image counts. And it is important to remember that image is not what you see in the mirror, it's what others see when they look at you, and usually in the first thirty seconds. First impressions are important, and that is the reason you should give primary consideration to the way you dress.

The same rules apply for both men and women regarding color, line, etc. Women who want to be perceived as upwardly mobile should wear classic dresses or suits; men should wear dark suits; with some concession to climate. For both men and women, a diagonal line is the best line you can wear. Women can find this line in jacket cuts; men most often in ties. The most important "no-no" for men is to avoid combining checks and prints at one time.

You can be innovative. Chrysler chairman Lee Iococca legitimized the contrast-collar shirt: white collar with a striped shirt. And Ronald Reagan wears brown suits, *not* the color of choice in 1976, when *Dress for Success* was first published. (Sequels include *The Women's Dress for Success Book* and *Live For*

Success.) Brown was thought to be a negative color for men who were perceived as either too strong or too weak. But Reagan, who has made it to the top, looks "very good" in brown, according to Molloy.

In surveys done using photographs of the same person in various attire, the subjects were typified as being blue-collar or white-collar; executive or not, based merely on the clothing they wore. Know this, and use this knowledge to build your wardrobe.

Dress for the Occasion

If you really want to make an impact, you need to dress for the occasion. If you want to know what that occasion calls for, look to the powerful people who usually attend. It is not only important to dress well, but it is essentially important to be noticed, and that means in a quiet, non-conspicuous way. As Molloy says, "Other people want you to look pleasant and attractive rather than self-confident and authoritative."

Of course, various industries have standards that may be more conservative or elaborate. You would not expect a corporate lawyer to dress the same way a Hollywood film producer does, and they don't. Advertising executives and other so-called "creative types" dress less formally than bankers. You certainly do not not want to be considered the "oddball" of whatever group you are in. Molloy feels you should "cater to the instincts of the person you work for," especially if you want to be promoted, and if you know what your boss values.

I have always followed two basic rules during the time that I taught Image, and I think they can still be relied on today. They are the Color Rule and the Rule of Eight.

The Color Rule
You should never wear more than three colors at one time, with the third color being neutral (black, white, beige, gray). Usually when black or white is used as a main color, only wear one other. When there are several colors represented in one piece of fabric (print, plaid, stripes) it will only count as three colors.

The Rule of Eight

Everything you have on that is visible to another person counts as 1 point if it is a single color, 2 points if it is two colors, and 3 points if it is three colors. Since nothing can be more than three colors, no item can be worth more than 3 points. Two pieces of matching jewelry count 1; three pieces of matching jewelry count 2. Individual, unmatched pieces count as 1 each. Jewelry worn daily such as watches, wedding rings, etc., are not counted. But separate belts of a fabric different than your ensemble do count. Textured or opaque hose is counted. Now what does all this mean? *You should never have on less than 6 points or you are underdressed, and never more than 8 points or you are overdressed.* Briefcases and handbags are not included. If you have a question about how you are dressed, add it up.

Making Your Entrance

Walking, sitting and standing are not easy to do if you know everyone is watching you, so practice all of these basics. Make sure your shoes are comfortable, and pause 30 seconds before entering a room where you plan to do any kind of business. Study the room and how you will negotiate it. Do not sit in a couch or chair if getting up will be at all difficult. Make eye contact, one of the most assertive things you can do.

As much as physical poise, you will need to have vocal poise to handle yourself in group situations. As difficult as it may be, you need to develop some mastery over the fine art of small talk. One simple way is by reading. You should read one book a month, a newspaper on a daily basis and a professional or trade magazine weekly. This will keep you informed and give you a confident base from which to speak.

Of course, none of this matters without the proper attitude, enthusiasm and personality. Someone with an outstanding personality can make everyone around them feel good whether he is wearing the right clothes or not.

How can you nurture this attitude? First, by liking yourself, and making time for yourself, to restore and recharge and improve yourself. You need time to read, to shop, to think, to watch football games or listen to music or do whatever it is that periodically takes you out of yourself.

Eat Right; Exercise For Vigor; and Like Yourself

This is not a diet book, but diet is important to your well-being; and it is hard to have a good self-image if you are drastically out of shape. Your attitude will improve with effort, as long as you don't get too unrealistic about it. Remember it takes 3,500 calories to make a pound, so if you have pounds to gain or lose, it will take time. Losing 25 pounds in one month may be unrealistic; but not 25 pounds in one year. That's only a half-pound a week, and any good scale will tell you how you are doing.

Exercise in the form of games are good at any age, but if you need to alter a specific part of your body, you may need to take a diet/exercise program aimed at this change. Unfair as it may be, people ascribe attitudes to you which may or may not be true based on nothing more than appearance. Make sure those attitudes are ones you want associated with your name. If not, change your image.

Successful people come in all shapes and sizes. Actor Danny DeVito is only five feet tall, which is five inches taller than sex therapist Dr. Ruth Westheimer. And Dustin Hoffman is only five-foot-six. Obviously, you cannot stretch to greater heights in a physical way, but you can use what you have, if you like what you have.

Trade your self-consciousness in for assertiveness. Being assertive does not mean stepping on others to get your own way, it means that you take charge of your life and avoid having others make important decisions for you. Free yourself from self-consciousness by honestly evaluating your skills. Neither overrate nor underrate your assets. One of those assets, obviously, is your appearance. Maximize it by looking and acting confident.

When you look your best, you can do your best. And doing your best can, and will, take you to the top.

CHAPTER 6
Body Language and Winning Impressions

"Trifles make perfection. And perfection is no trifle."
—Michaelangelo

Truly understanding how we communicate is essential to developing a winning image. Did you know that fifty-five percent of all communication is body language? That statistic comes from a classic study on nonverbal communication conducted by Albert Mehrabian.

Some of his other findings are equally interesting. Mehrabian discovered that, besides the heavy consideration listeners give to the body language of a speaker, 38 percent of what people responded to was vocal tone, and only 7 percent were the actual words of the message. The subjects of his study were asked to describe, in turn, a message on video with no sound, a typed transcript of the same message, and a recording which made the words incomprehensible but still retained the tone of voice.

Additionally, he found that *whenever any nonverbal behavior contradicted the verbal, it was the nonverbal part of the message that was most likely to determine the impact of the message.* Touching, spatial relationships between speaker and listener, eye contact, postures, gestures, and facial and vocal expressions dominate any actual words said. In this study, as in business as a whole, it's not what you say, it's how you say it.

Body language is important more as an awareness factor than anything else. It does give off impressions to others, so you need to be aware of the various signals you are sending. But it is also important not to misinterpret. When someone crosses their arms, it may mean that they are being defensive (the classic interpretation), or it may mean they are cold. Usually when someone uses the "steepling" position with their fingertips, it means they are calm and in control. However, it could just as well indicate boredom.

When you combine body language with the actual scene of involvement, it takes on a deeper meaning. If you approach my office, poke your head in and ask, "Do you have a minute?" and I put my pen down, lean back in the chair and invite you in, I have indicated I have both the time and interest to deal with you at that moment. If, however, you approach me the same way and I look up, pen in hand, and do not change position, I am indicating I am busy and may have 30 seconds at best.

Good body language, which gives off the appropriate message at the appropriate time, goes a long way toward making the proper impression—whether it is in the board room, an office situation with a peer, or in addressing a group. The turn of a shoulder, a down-cast look to the eyes, a sullen stare all give off messages, and these messages play an important role, especially in negotiations, which we will have more to say about later.

Making a Winning Impression

Winning impressions are derived from many different factors. The way you dress and carry yourself, your speech and vocabulary, your fitness and energy level. But it also comes from your ability to fit in when necessary and stir up a rumble when that is called for. It is important not to be a 'yes' person. Playing the devil's advocate is also not necessarily bad. It may fuel a needed discussion. People respect you when your opinion is worthwhile. That is why it is so important to make sure that when you open your mouth, you have something important to say.

A winning impression often means being known as a member of the team who backs his teammates and goes out on a limb for them, and it also means standing up for one's own beliefs when necessary, even if they are different from the majority. To make a winning impression, you must have convictions as well as charisma, vision as well as vitality, and persistence as well as the ability to react quickly.

These qualities also describe a leader. In order to lead, there must be someone who will follow—and people will only follow if they have someone they admire and respect as well as someone who has the ability to win. People do like being on the winning side—it *is* the American Dream.

When people see you anywhere—eating in a restaurant, running through the airport, stopped at a red light—do you look like a winner? When you make a presentation at your company, turn in an assignment, attend an association meeting, suggest an idea—do you do it like a winner? Do you play to win, or play not to lose?

In their excellent book, *The Winning Performance: How America's High-Growth Midsize Companies Succeed* authors Donald K. Clifford, Jr. and Richard E. Cavanagh discussed four themes shared in the management styles of more than 6,000 CEOs of companies which grew at a rate between three and four times faster than the national average. These qualities relate directly to winning impressions, because the numbers are on the board.

These winning companies preached a philosophy of *earned respect* , that the business was special because of what it stands for, what it does and how it does it. And, because it is special, the thinking continues, it deserves extra effort from those who work there.

Leaders of these companies also shared what the authors called *evangelical zeal*—an honest enthusiasm that spills over to those with whom the enterprise does business, from employees and prospective employees through customers, suppliers, distributors and *even competitors.*

These CEOs were not avaricious. Instead, they viewed profit and the creation of wealth as *inevitable by-products of doing other things well* .

Most important, these winning CEOs shared a *habit of dealing people in*—the tradition of communicating just about everything to just about everybody in the organization and enfranchising them as partners in the crusade. Strategies, plans, ambitions and problems are not the secrets of the palace guard; they are known and appreciated throughout the company.

Leadership can be a learned skill, and a powerful way of making an impression. Leaders are not born, they are developed. Choose to be on the winning side. Grow, develop, experience and become the person you have always wanted to be. Take risks, make decisions, investigate, experiment, these are all learning processes, and you'll be making a winning impresssion each step of the way.

CHAPTER 7
Winning the Battle of the Sexes

"Who says you can't have it all?"

—Slogan in a beer commercial

In the late 1980s, men and women who are successful in business need to be sensitive to the needs, wants and "conditioning" of the opposite sex as at no other time in this or any other nation's history. People want more out of the workplace in terms of sexual freedom (which certainly includes freedom from sexual harassment or stereotyping) and the freedom to play complex and often contradictory roles. It may require some of the same skills to run a corporation as it does to bring up a family and balance a budget, but it certainly requires some shifting of gears. Just as children do not want "Mom the boss," workers may not respond well to "boss the Mom."

Women want, and deserve but do not yet get, equal pay for equal work. And men do not want to be seen as the "heavies" in this or any other oppression of women. The bottom line is, we all have choices. We do decide which job we accept, whom to marry, whether or not to continue our education, whether to stay in a dead-end job, and even whether to stay in the same geographical locale. The hard part is realizing that we have indeed made our own beds, and must lie in them.

True, there are sometimes circumstances that prevent us from making a move at a particular moment. But over a longer period, say five to 10 years, a way will appear in which to change our path, if we sincerely desire to do so.

That is when it becomes important to intensely evaluate what our direction and priorities are, to set meaningful goals and pursue them in a disciplined way. Only after looking at all options, assets, liabilities and stumbling blocks can you decide what is important. *The* most important step is action. Do not over-analyze. Go with what you know. If you want change and you want to make something happen, you must take action.

It is true that my life is unique. As an entrepreneur, I have been able to make my own decisions, but it was my choice to be me. And it was my choice to take the risks that go along with owning your own business. It was not an easy road to follow, and there were plenty of days of worry. There still are. But I preferred the worry and problems over what I considered the rigid structure of another kind of world.

Can you have it all—marriage, family, career? The odds are against it. In today's environment, a child has a better than even chance of being raised by somone other than his two natural parents. The nuclear family is already a near-myth, and it is threatened by many of the things we are talking about in this book: success, the individual's need for recognition and self-fulfillment which may come from a variety of sources. Speaking for myself, a whole lot of it comes from my husband and children.

I feel I have found the perfect mate, but I can say without hesitation that were he not perfect for me, I would not be married. I observed him and learned a lot about him before we were married. I knew not to get married with the idea of changing someone. Whatever they are like before you say "I do" is a good indication of how they will be later. Fortunately, we have grown together, not apart, while developing totally different careers and viewpoints. Since the question often comes from women, let me speak to their concerns first.

Back to the Future

There are absolutely no housewife heroines anymore. Look at television (for proof, not for inspiration). Women are doctors, lawyers, heads of detective agencies, gun-toting crime-stoppers.

They do not wait, as they did in days gone by, for the man to bring home the paycheck. And neither do the women who watch these shows. What can create problems in the real world, however, is if you have been a devoted wife and mother and then decide to return to work. It's hard for you—you will likely need additional training and may be competing with women much younger than yourself. And it can be hard on your family.

The problem gets compounded when the work becomes more and more interesting, and therefore, more important. Disaster can strike when the job becomes a career because of your competency and progression. Is this fair? Of course not. Is it real? For many families whose "lady of the house" is no longer in, it is.

Researchers at Stanford University found in 1987 that husbands of working mothers experience more stress than any other group of men, married or single. Is it really any surprise? They are experiencing the greatest shift in expectations of any population group in the country. And money is no salve for stress. Relieving stress, as will be explained in the next chapter, is one of the keys to success for any individual, or couple, on the way up.

At the point your career begins to define itself, a lot depends on your husband. Is he a secure person? If he is, he won't feel threatened. If not, then look out—he won't lift one finger at home to help out, and will expect you to do everything you did pre-job. His reaction will have a great influence on the children. If they see he has accepted what you do with pride, they will most likely feel the same way and pitch right in. Of course, if you have worked from the very beginning, the children will accept your work as part of the natural course of things, which is another motivation if you care about instilling a value for work in your children.

Other problems include the extra-curricular activities that go along with your career choice. I have often said that if women, or men, are going to make it in the business world, they're not going to do it by working eight-hour days. You've got to go early and come home late, and maybe bring work with you even then. Ten- to twelve-hour-days are more realistic. You must be aware of the strain this puts on your family, especially if they are accustomed to having you there at set times.

If your work requires you to attend professional organizational meetings (in the evening), conventions (out-of-town), dinner meetings with clients (especially if they're men) and various other time consumers, the red light may go on in a hurry and a choice may have to be made. A great deal depends on your basic relationship with your husband and how badly you want it to survive.

Money or a lack of it can cut both ways. In her book, *Stress and the Healthy Family* author Dolores Curran says the number one cause of stress for both men and women of *all* economic classes is **money**. There is never enough. Although your husband may be aware of the need for you to work so the bills can be paid, or a down-payment can be met, once this is accomplished, he may feel you've done enough. On the other hand, if you begin to earn more money than he does, he may never be able to accept it. And face it, would you want him to? Masculine pride does get in the way sometimes. Tempers can become strained when finances are tight, however. So be prepared.

Now, suppose you survive that hurdle with family and career intact, what do you find? Increasingly, although the top positions in nearly every industry are held by men, women are breaking through.

In 1986, women who graduated with a Master of Business Administration degree from the University of Pennsylvania's Wharton School of Business, started at salaries averaging 1.3 percent more than their male counterparts. However, farther up the ladder, women above vice-presidential level who are making more than $124,000 a year are still earning 42 percent less than their male colleagues. Nearly a quarter of all MBA graduates are women, more than double the number ten years ago. For women in management, the push is definitely on.

Despite current inequities, I think women are doing quite well. If you compare the number of women in senior management and the length of time they have been in the field with men, the ratio becomes more favorable. In another 30 years, women in top management assure me, they will be well represented. If you feel you are not progressing as you should, because of antiquated ideas about what a women can or cannot do, your choice is clear: Make a change or bite the bullet.

A Word for Men: Expect Competition

For men, the situation is different. Few young men today come from the traditional family where the mother stayed at home and kept house. Growing up with women in their graduate classes, in organizations and trade associations, most younger men are able to deal with a woman in the workplace whether she is peer, boss or subordinate. They feel comfortable, non-threatened and usually experience no hostility in return. My youngest son *expects* women to succeed and to be his competition. That is how he grew up.

There is still, however, a "good old boy" network, but it is slowly dying out, and the savvy male of today knows better than to discriminate because of sex. If he marries, he will likely need a working wife to be able to afford the home they want and the education for their children. Men also expect to pitch in with child care and household chores, although many are still tradition-bound in which chores they will do. The "house husband" is still a rarity.

With most men today, roles are not the issue. Successful coupling of people on the way to the top usually involves a meshing of philosophies, lifestyles and goals. Many couples have agreed to the contract, "whoever's career gets the opportunity first is the one we go with." Many of my female friends have received job offers in other cities and their husbands have picked up and moved with them. That was unheard of a generation ago.

Whether you are a man or a woman, the only real way to come out ahead is to follow your own path—working in the field you choose for an organization you admire and following your code of ethics in a manner you are comfortable with. You must learn to get along with most people, whether you admire their style or not. You need to follow orders as well as give them, and most important you must stick to your guns, your ideals and ethical standards. You will not come out ahead through antagonizing or alienating. Sooner or later, someone who complains all the time will be considered a complainer—not a team player.

What Is a Team Player?

"Team player" is an '80s buzzword. But what does it really mean? When I talk about a team player, I mean someone who knows the score and plays accordingly. I am certainly a loner in terms of business and doing, but I am a team player in trade and social organizations, and any partnerships. The trick is knowing when to play which role, and the time to play with the team is when the chips are down, and everyone needs to pull together. Sometimes, for the team to win, exceptional individual performances are required, and if you are alert to those opportunities, you will be able to shine in the knowledge that you *and the team* did their best.

Keep your eyes and ears open for opportunities that present themselves—and they will. You come out ahead by being prepared, in experience, talent, abilities and attitude.

I have, thankfully, not encountered much discrimination in my life. In college, I started out at a large university where I found there was no chance for "hands-on" work until my junior or senior year. I did not waste my energies trying to change a rigid system. I transferred to a college where you could be anything you wanted from the day you arrived—and it was wonderful. There was no discrimination based on sex or class or major or anything else. If you were good enough, you were given a chance.

There are opportunities like this all over. You just have to look for them. You can make excuses all of your life about why things won't work, or you can begin to look for all the ways they *will* work. Nothing is easy, and everything worthwhile usually takes a little longer, but the people who try, and try well, consistently, day after day and week after week, doing an excellent job each and every time they perform their task, will make it.

A positive attitude may be a very simplistic way to approach adversity, but when coupled with persistence and skill, it can be a very powerful influence, can help your image, and can boost you closer to the top.

CHAPTER 8
Handling Stress and Time

"Here is a test to find whether your mission on earth is finished: If you're alive, it isn't."

—Richard Bach

It has been proven that five minutes of negative thinking takes 24 hours to recover from. How many of us have 24 hours to throw away? Remember Norman Cousins, the editor of *Saturday Review?* He was diagnosed as having a terminal disease. He said he was not going to die and he locked himself in a hotel room for three and a half months. He slept only four hours a night. The other twenty hours he showed himself Laurel and Hardy, Three Stooges and Marx Brothers movies, and he did nothing but laugh. And his illness is *still* in remission. Healing laughter does a tremendous amount to reduce stress. Remember it is difficult to have clenched teeth when you smile, and you cannot be tense if your teeth are not clenched. A positive attitude is so necessary. Aren't there people you don't want to say, "How are you?" to because they'll tell you for thirty minutes?

High Demands Plus No Control Equals Stress

Stress doesn't come from too many hours of work or not getting what you want. Stress comes from *high demands and no control.* This is an important lesson for supervisors as well as those in the trenches. When you have no say in things that are really important to you, and yet you are required to produce anyway—that is where frustration starts to build. It increases to the danger zone when you realize that you do not make a difference; when you have a really fantastic idea that is not being listened to; when you are not considered as an individual. Dangerous to whom? To everyone. A burned-out employee does not have a happy life at home, or a productive life on the job.

That is where assertive management comes in. You need to listen to your people and hear what they're saying. You must find an outlet for their ideas and suggestions. When you stop listening and the company doesn't care, there is no motivation for the employees. When there is no motivation yet high demands are still called for, stress results.

Step 1: Name Your Stressors

Identify your stressors. These come in various sizes and shapes, they can be human or not, they can be situations or events—related to family, job or school. Or it can be a combination of things. What causes stress in one person may not even be noticed by someone else. That is why we can never judge anyone else's circumstance. We must always try to understand and be tolerant. Go to a quiet place and think about the things that get you upset, frustrated, and tense. At a recent management seminar, one of the participants said he had recently undergone a double bypass operation. He was fairly young, about 32, and I was surprised. He went on to say that his doctor had identified his stressor as his immediate boss and told him he had two choices. He could either die, or quit his job. He didn't quit, but he did move to a different department. He had a stress test and was told he was in fine shape. That story points out what a bad superior can do to you. I am sure if a boss can do that to an employee, an employee or a group of employees could do it to a boss as well.

Step 2: Reduce the Load

Stress is a result of mental overload. That is why it is important to keep everything in perspective and to exert assertiveness. Use techniques like self-disclosure and workable compromise. Self-disclosure is usually an "I" statement. Never accuse people with a "you" statement. When you say "I think," "I feel"—you are positioning yourself. Remember, assertiveness is believing you have the right to state your thoughts, feelings and opinions as long as they are not hostile. Workable compromise is getting to a "win-win" which is what negotiation is all about. It is the willingness to give a little on both sides when you really want something to work.

State your reactions to any situation in a positive way. If you don't reduce the overload that comes from holding feelings in, you will not be able to deal with the stress and you are just prolonging the problem. The classic reaction to stress in the past has either been fight or flight. Flight is to withdraw and not deal with it in a classic non-assertive or passive mode; quit or change jobs or departments without regard for self.

The fight response means you lash out at anyone or anything around you. Usually this can produce high blood pressure, depression and various other afflictions. Psychological stress can trigger hormonal changes as well as physiological ailments. Problems occur when stressful situations happen one after the other, such as problems on the job on a daily basis or going home at night to an unhappy marriage or when there is never enough money to pay the bills on a weekly cycle no matter how much you skrimp and save. Since we know that lack of assertive communication is responsible for most problems of stress on the job, we must continue to practice the assertive techniques just mentioned.

The Deadly One Hundred

We all experience approximately 100 abrasive incidents a day, from hostility on the highway to unwelcome telephone solicitations. Abrasive incidents may come in disguise. If you are the person who works 12 hours a day because you can't get anyone else to do it, or takes no for an answer because no one else will do it. Those are abrasive incidents. Don't become hostile. Don't strike out. All are stress builders. When you start to become anxious about something, it is usually a sign. Become aware. Let people know where you stand. Their reaction may surprise you. They like it because it gives them more control, and therefore less stress.

You cannot have control if you do not know who and what your stressors are. We must know to avoid them in the future or change them, if possible. We must also find ways to deal with our stress so that we can cope effectively. Assertive management and attitude have a lot to do with coping and how people perceive us. The mind can imagine stress where it isn't. Be aware and take care.

Assertive management is one way to reduce stress. Stress cannot be avoided in this day and age. There is too much change and restructuring going on all the time. There is nothing so constant these days as change. And since change is a primary fear in people's lives, it is something we have to learn to deal with. Major factors are the amount of stress, its length and your perception of it. Not all stress is negative.

Stress Can Be Positive

Positive stress prepares us for the event that is going to happen. It usually gives us the ability to perform and follow through. It's what allows an athlete to perform while injured or tired, a mother to lift unrealistic amounts of weight to save her child, a performer to get though a show all right—all the things to which you say, 'I don't know how I did that'—but you did. Positive stress spurs us on and makes us better and stronger. It is negative stress that we have to guard against. That is what drains our energy and dries us out. That is what causes headaches, tension and a weary feeling. All this works toward more aggravation because most of today's stresses are emotional, prompted by outside influences, often manufactured or magnified by the person under stress.

It is not the situation that causes stress but our handling of it. Some people thrive on challenges. If they didn't have conflict they would be bored. But they do view it as a challenge, not a problem. Others like to throw a monkey wrench into a plan just to see what happens.

Tensions and anxieties may make us work harder, but not

necessarily smarter. In 1986, stress cost companies in the United States $17 *billion*. The cost per employee is about $1,250 per person. That's a lot of money spent on something that can be controlled by an individual through changing thought processes and lifestyle.

There are many sources of stress but a major one for working people is having no direction in the workplace. Ambiguity in communication, responsibility with no authority, conflicting demands and too many projects with no clue of what is most important—all heighten the sense of stress. If you couple this with no recreation or leisure life, and an unsteady home environment, you are usually headed straight for trouble. If you find yourself in a highly compromising situation because you are faced with a decision you don't want to make or a report that is unpleasant, or a peer who has not performed, you will usually experience stress. The demands keep rising as the control slips away. Pain and tension are the usual physical results.

Relief Is Just a Deep Breath Away

An effective stress reduction technique is deep breathing. No one will necessarily notice you doing this, but what a difference it makes. It should calm you down as well as increase your energy flow. It also gives you a chance to rethink what you might want to say, and to observe what else is going on around you.

Another stress reducer is honesty. If you tell the truth, you usually eliminate the problem of trying to remember what you said. Trying to keep stories straight can be a full-time project. Honesty is usually the best policy and when people start requesting a cover-up, that's when you should start reevaluating your position. If what other people do impacts you negatively, then you have to do something about changing that situation. That may mean a position, a boss, a company, or a friend. You, of course, should always try to negotiate. But if that doesn't work or you wind up having to do all the giving, the change should occur. Of course, there are people who will never make a change because they are fearful or in a rut. Or because of parent tapes or because they are just plain lazy and don't want to help themselves.

Try to receive criticism openly and don't become defensive. Just because people don't agree with you or make alternate suggestions doesn't mean they are your enemies or are trying to belittle you. Welcome it warmly and with good spirit. Don't create further feelings of resentment and hostility. Do not look for approval in everything you do or you will cause yourself great disappointment. If you want to be a leader, dare to be different, even a little radical, and don't expect everyone to go along with you. If you are looking for everyone—peer, subordinate, and superior—to think you are neat in every decision and absolutely perfect, it just won't happen. That can be very destructive to you and can hinder your progress as a manager.

Assertive Management: Playing to Win-Win

Be prepared to take some risks. But remember, we are trying to get to a win-win. Don't put anyone in a losing position purposely. If you deal only with the facts up front, you will find a much less tension-filled atmosphere. No one can argue with what is. Do not get drawn into personal arguments or situations. You must learn to differentiate behavior from personality. Try not to dislike someone on their style, or words. Look beneath for the reason why. And if you still think this person is an undesirable character, so be it. Don't think that the sun rises or sets on this situation. When someone or some thing controls you that much it cannot be for the good. The main point you need to remember is that you are a professional. And if you look and act like one no one can tear you down. Judge people on their competence, just as you would wish them to judge you. Don't get hung up on idiosyncracies. You cannot be all things to all people, and neither can anyone else.

You should find out how the game is played. Know who the power people are and who not to cross. Follow the leaders and see how they act, dress and perform. Observe their thinking process and find out why things are done the way they are. Learn how to be in the mainstream rather than out of flux. Get a mentor. Support your peers. Help your subordinates, listen to your superiors, network. Use your contacts, and always keep an open mind.

Assertive management lends itself to today's healthy attitudes. We all know that today's consumers are better educated, more aware, and certainly more sophisticated than ever before. At no other time have they had more rights, or more champions in their corners. They want quality and they want service, the first time. And they deserve it. Assertive people are adult in their dealings and they are not prejudiced by people's tantrums or machinations. They are usually in control and have self-esteem. By being themselves they will inspire confidence.

Assertive managers are not afraid to give. They will coach, counsel and motivate because they know by doing this they will create a better system. This system will produce more with less problems and tension, and this in turn will reflect back on them in an extremely positive light. It is a win-win all the way around, because their employees will be excited and will want to do a better job because they are being rewarded and recognized. This is reflected in attitude and performance, and then profits. You can't ask for much more than that.

Enjoy this aspect of management. It will definitely spiral you up the ladder of success. You will achieve just about everything you want. Just remember. Respect yourself, your peers, your coworkers, your superiors and all your contemporaries, and good management and lifestyle will be yours.

Start to keep track of the individuals and people who are causing you stress. Is it because they are disagreeing with you; do you feel as if you are losing control? Are other people putting you on the defensive? Take a look at your diet, too. Is there any time in your day scheduled for something other than work and personal duties?

Reduce Stress By Making More Time

I feel that time management can lead to greater productivity, less stress and pressure, and more creativity. In addition, knowing one is more organized and in control adds to confidence, enthusiasm and flexibility.

Remember, if you only pick up 30 minutes a day, that represents 22 more eight-hour days. In the working world, that is an entire month.

You can read all you want about time management. But unless you are willing to go though a behavior modification to replace bad habits with good, nothing will happen.

The first thing you need to do is make a time log. I suggest you do the log in 15 or 30 minute increments, for two reasons. During that time write down exactly what you have accomplished, and if you were interrupted by the phone five times or six people came into your office, note that. After two weeks, you will notice a pattern forming, and you will be able to determine whether you have quiet time available, slower periods when traffic through your office or department is less, or whether you need more control over what you do. Regardless, you will learn something from it and you will be able to start scheduling in time for you.

The time log should be discontinued after two weeks, and repeated quarterly just to be sure you are on track and don't begin slipping.

Plan your day the night before. This allows you to walk through your day and have a good idea what it contains. You must have your priorities and objectives set before you get to the office. If the first working hour of your day is not a productive one, your entire day will go poorly. I am sure you have said more than once, "It looks like it is going to be one of those days." Usually that happens because your priorities were not clear, objectives not set, and someone else has interrupted and controlled your time. You also need to know your biological time clock. Are you a night person or a day person? Some people are up at 6 a.m. and jogging. Others need fourteen cups of coffee to get them going. Others function extremely well at night, and like taking work home with them.

Use Your Prime Time

The idea is to do your most difficult projects during your prime hours. If you try to tackle them during your worst times, you will find yourself procrastinating. You must also learn to prioritize.

Most management books talk about A, B and C priorities. I term A priorities those which are both *urgent and important*.

They must be done within this 24 hour period. B's are either important but not urgent, or urgent but not important. They can be put off until tomorrow. C's hopefully will go away all by themselves.

Once you determine what the priority is, you must rank order it, such as A-1, A-2, A-3 and so forth. You must not veer from this determination once it is made, because this ensures that you always work on the most important project first. You may never get to a 2 priority because of interruptions or your job functions, but at least you will have worked on your primary target. Most of us get sidetracked by working on the easiest things first, or we move from one chore to the other with no clear plan. We figure it is simpler to get the little things out of the way. The problem with this is we never get to our important items; we become busy with activities rather than results. We can always keep ourselves busy, but are we accomplishing anything?

Write everything down. Since we only remember 40 percent of what we want to on time, it is imperative that we commit things to paper. Fortunately, people do this, but on little pieces of paper which get scattered, are distracting and sometimes even get thrown in the trash. The worst thing that has happened to us are the yellow sticky pieces of paper which have found their way into our lives. You find them stuck to everything: desks, lamps, drawers, walls—even ourselves. They are great when sending a memo to someone which is attached to an object; this way the message doesn't get lost. But when they are all over your work area, they will boggle your mind.

You need to commit your thoughts, "to do's," reminders and projects to a single sheet of paper. It is much easier to keep track of a single sheet than several small pieces of paper, and far less distracting. I strongly recommend this for telephone messages as well. It is absolutely the most horrible feeling to come back from lunch and see forty-two pink slips waiting for you. It is all right to return the messages from the pink slips if you are going to do it right there. But if you are going to wait, or once you've made the initial attempt to return the calls, they must be placed on a single sheet of paper. Believe me, you will come to a great realization that this is best once you find it relieves you of stress and tension, and you are able to see things at a glance. It gives you more control, and that is what you are looking for.

Set Realistic Deadlines, and Stick to Them

Learn to set realistic deadlines and honor them. Every project or task needs to have one; it gives you a framework in which to work. It also allows you to budget the time in small increments to reach that deadline. The average administrator is interrupted every six minutes. It is therefore important to divide projects into five, ten and fifteen-minute segments. It relieves procrastination, and will create more productivity. If you find yourself simply overloaded continually, you have three basic choices: delegate, come in early, leave late and skip lunch, or change your priorities from A to B. There are no other ways. You must make a value choice as to what works for you.

Most time management gurus tell you to touch a piece of paper only once. I don't believe that can happen. But I do believe that a decision can be made on every piece of paper that comes into your life. Don't put it to one side or it will be the first of a pile, and before you know it it will have grown and taken over. Your paper goes to three places: the trash, a file, or you route it to someone else. It should never create a new, visible distraction. Ninety percent of filed paper is never referred to again. It may need to be stored for legal or record-keeping processes, but it should be out of the way.

Keep Goals Handy

One piece of paper you don't want to file away is your goals statement. Everyone needs written goals. Having them run around in your head with no plan of action will do you no good. You must have them clearly visible, so that when people come by to distract you, you can look at your list and see if it has anything to do with what you have planned for the day. If you honestly evaluate how your day is used, you will find that 80 percent of it has nothing to do with where you want to go in life. Your activities must be linked to your goals, but results are what's important.

Try to set one major objective a day, and reach it. Remember, you are the one who puts the importance on the objective, no one else.

Negative thinking will produce negative results. Napolean Hill, author of *Think and Grow Rich* said, "What the mind can conceive, the mind will believe." Think about how you can improve five minutes a day, then ten, then fifteen.

Today's etiquette allows you some timesavers. For example, you can now reply to a letter with a handwritten note on the original. You can save space in your files by putting a copy of the typed reply on the back of the original letter sent to you, thereby having one sheet of paper instead of two. You can color-code files to go by subjects, divisions and so forth. None of these things are major, but they all save time. And those minutes add up at the end of the day.

If you are supervising people, I strongly suggest you start off each day with a 15-minute meeting so that you can keep them on track, so that they can give you feedback on their personal dilemmas, and everyone will be operating on the same wavelength. Unfortunately, priorities change from one day to the next.

Interestingly, most interruptions are within the company, so they are controllable. If I know I can call you at any time and get an answer, I will continue to do it.

Log Interruptions, Too

Keep an interruption log, so you will know the time of day they are the heaviest, and who the most bothersome culprit is. Wouldn't it be interesting to find your boss is coming in to see you ten or fifteen times a day, and then wants to know why you aren't more productive? Or, perhaps your secretary keeps running in for little things that she should be making the decision on—if you have given her the authority, that is. Knowing how insidious interruptions are may make you more courteous. For sure, it will give you a way to document the people and the problems that are breaking up your day.

Set aside some part of your day for physical fitness. Although there is no proof your life will be longer, your life will be better if you exercise. Take at least 30 minutes for some type of movement, whether it's aerobics, walking, jogging, swimming, racquetball or whatever.

Concentrate on one important thing at a time, Don't let your ideas vanish. Keep them in an idea book that you can refer back to; don't lose those important thoughts, but don't get sidetracked by them.

You must also believe you are doing an effective job, or you won't continue to perform. If you don't like a task, you will certainly find a lot of ways to get out of it.

Don't make a resolution that you will suddenly become a time expert. It won't happen. But you can begin by preparing adequately for things. You can make some headway every day. You can begin to control more of what is going on around you. Then suddenly you will have five minutes more, then ten, then fifteen.

Paperwork is usually a means to an end. Don't let it become a focal point of your life. Your desk should be fairly clear. In truth, you only need three files on your desk. One is a reading file for you to put important memos, articles and so forth into; a projects file for those important happenings and a correspondence file for answers. Since I have no secretary, I accumulate a minimum of five pieces of correspondence, and then I answer them. Believe it or not, it takes the same amount of time to respond to five as one.

The Time Bank System

Have a collection of 1 through 31 loose-leaf pages, representing the days of the month. Everything you have to do is put down on one of these pages, then prioritized A, B or C as we have discussed, and then ranked A-1, A2, A-3. Those things not done must be either moved ahead to another day or crossed off as no longer important. Nothing is left unattended. So when someone says they will call you, or something is coming in the mail, you now have a place to put it.

Every seven days you remove the used seven days in front and add seven pages in back, so you always have 30 days at a time to work with. At the end of each day, everything must be crossed off, or put on another page of your 1-31 section. If you put everything down on these pages, you will begin to clear the clutter from your mind. Once you don't have to keep all these details in your head, your mind will become free to be creative.

Any name, address or phone number that you have to look up more than once will be recorded in an A-to-Z section in the notebook. So this becomes a walking Rolodex file.

How To Save On Meetings

Meetings are another time-waster. They should not be held when there is no purpose, and especially when there is no agenda. All meetings must adhere to the agenda which should have been given to all attendees previously, so they could prepare their input and a time frame should be referenced. Meetings should start and end on time, and have a goal targeted no matter how simply stated.

Twenty Timely Tips

1. Begin with a time log and discover your strengths and weaknesses.

2. Plan your day the night before so you get off to a good start.

3. Discover your prime hours so you schedule effectively.

4. Prioritize and rank your "to do" list.

5. Write everything down, even the things you are sure you will never forget.

6. Put all telephone messages on a single sheet of paper so they will be easier to work with.

7. Set deadlines for everything.

8. Make a decision on each piece of paper, and place papers in one of your three files or discard or reroute them. Don't create piles.

9. Set goals for yourself and achieve them.

10. Have a 15-minute daily meeting with your staff.

11. Think positively.

12. Learn shortcuts.

13. Handle interruptions effectively by knowing who, and what, they are.

14. Take time for physical fitness. It will give you more energy.

15. Learn to focus and concentrate.

16. Eliminate paperwork. Don't let it control you.

17. Use single sheets for record-keeping on people and products.

18. Use a 1-through-31 section for your "to do" list.

19. File all current product, project and people sheets in your A-though-Z section.

20. Keep meetings on track.

Using dead time is a skill. If you place a value on your time, you will have more of it, and less stress. The result will be more confidence and competence and a richer, fuller life.

Part III: *Winning Communications*

CHAPTER 9
Face-to-Face Versus Over the Telephone

"Every person in your organization is within an arm's reach of the most profitable power tool in the business."
—George R. Walther, from his book *"Phone Power"*

A friend of ours is fond of saying, "I know if I can get the interview, I've got the job." Perhaps you know someone who feels the same way about sales. That kind of confidence is admirable, but it helps to be able to back it up with results. Can you make the sale, whether that sale is yourself or a product, once you have the face-to-face interview? Do you have the telephone skills to get that interview? Your appearance, body language and ability to play whatever games are offered will speak volumes about your success here. But there is much more to winning communications than good looks and sharp dress.

Be Witty and Wise

Conversation is really the art which reveals much of the truth about people. It is the exchange of ideas and reflects your character, interest and experiences. It's the best way you can get to know other people, their interests and experiences, as well as to share yours.

If you have trouble with conversation, or consider it "small talk," consider how you feel about those people who talk to you in uncomfortable social situations. If you're like me, you're grateful to them for breaking the ice. Good conversations inspire confidence, build respect in business, school and social life, help make friends, develop distinct personalities and reveal your abilities to others.

The first rule of becoming a good conversationalist is: Be gracious. Never say anything which you will later regret. You can always say it later, but you can never take it back. Be lively and have a good presence of mind. Concentrate on what's being said. If you cannot remember what you are talking about, why should someone else? Have an idea book. If you read something interesting, jot it down. Then when you have a spare moment, say you're stuck in a strange town near a big library, pursue it further. If you want other people to be interested, be interesting. That's basic, and it's not difficult.

Remember when you accept a person's hospitality, you owe them two things. One is your attention, and two is your conversation. We need good conversation to survive. We all love candor, and despise lies and double-talk. It is through free and healthy conversation that we learn and exchange meaningful information.

That doesn't mean there are no taboos. It is wise to avoid religion, politics, race and sex as topics of conversation in social situations. But don't be so inhibited that you cease conversation altogether. Remember, shyness is a form of selfishness. If you are constantly thinking of yourself and your problems, you cannot think about anyone else.

Practice at home. Converse with your family members, and let them get to know you. Organize your thoughts, and don't let everything fly out all jumbly. Ask a question to get others talking. Hold family meetings, and practice your problem-solving techniques at home. Also practice your listening skills.

The best conversationalist is the person who can put the most people at ease at one time. He or she is not only interesting, but inspires others to be so. She speaks from the heart as well as the brain; is warm, simple, honest and human; she never lacks poise and is always at ease. She is a winner.

Love Thy Telephone

Unfortunately, most of us do most of our selling over the telephone, where our attention to details like dress and appearance tend not to matter. The telephone presents its own limitations and opportunities.

In my seminars on effective telephone communication, I teach that of all the skills employed when you speak on a telephone, the most basic ingredient is usually the hardest to keep in mind: common sense. The most important point in telephone use is that you must regard the telephone as a friend, and not an inconvenience. Once you begin to regard your phone as an information tool, your attitude will change for the better.

In a recent questionnaire, 15 percent of the respondents said they avoided using the telephone as much as possible, 51 percent showed no enthusiasm for using it as a business tool and only 33 percent, a mere one-third, said they enjoyed using it and would at every opportunity. Don't let the phone become something you avoid. Use it wisely and increase your business, solve your problems, get answers to your questions and give good service to your customers.

Let us look at what communication really is. True communication takes place when information is exchanged, understanding is promoted, and questions are answered. Of course, there are many barriers to communication that don't allow this to happen. They include culture, lifestyle and occupation.

Different cultures produce different dialects and languages which are extremely difficult to understand over the phone. This problem is heightened in bilingual cities like Miami or Montreal, or cosmopolitan cities like New York or Los Angeles. You may have to ask people to repeat, to slow down, and you will have to ask people to spell their names phonetically. Take the time.

Different words mean different things to different people. There are more than 18,000 words in our language with over 600,000 meanings. Even the same word in English is often interpreted differently by the British and the Americans. Although you should have a good command of the language, avoid using too many words. Don't use 50-cent words when nickel words will do. If you want to get most people where they live, keep the language simple.

The telephone can present some problems of its own. Since it is not a vehicle that allows us to interact on a face-to-face basis, there is no attachment developed between the parties. However, frequently phone contact between the same parties can produce a bond and a certain degree of loyalty.

It's more difficult to get good feedback over the phone. We have learned to filter out messages we know are likely to upset us. We all hear primarily what we want to, and nothing else. Distrust and suspicion are sometimes heightened by telephone callers who are trying to sell us something. If you have not been honest with me in the past, why should I trust you now? The famous line "the check is in the mail," is a good example. If it never has been in the past, chances are I will not believe it now. And of course, last, is the "WIIFM factor": What's In It For Me?

To counter these built-in limitations, effective telephone users must tailor their conversations positively. In giving feedback, it must be descriptive, not evaluative. It also needs to be specific, and not general. Too many times we accept answers that do not point out real problems. Learn to appreciate the needs of both the receiver and the sender. How each hears something depends on their communication style and their experiences, and background. Feedback should only be directed at something the person can change. They should not be made responsible for other people's problems. Hopefully, feedback will also be solicited and not imposed, and well-timed. Don't store up information for months, and then come down on somebody. Make sure all information is clear, concise and accurate.

Our confident saleswoman finds she is better off in a face-to-face encounter. It is difficult to be assertive over the telephone because we do not have eye contact. Therefore, we must rely on other skills, and sometimes they are not necessarily on target. Have you ever visualized the person you are dealing with over the telephone? The voice, the manner, the experience of the person have all come together for you to form a mental image of the individual you have come to know through this instrument. How many times have you been right? Or wrong?

Make Each Call Special

The phone is a powerful tool whose purpose is to help us achieve the results we want. One of the ways we do that is to treat it like a special occasion each and every time it rings. Not easy, I know. But important to remember.

Discipline is an important telephone skill. Not only do you

need some structure, but you also need to know how to make or accept a call, and how to end a call quickly, yet politely. Since 50 percent of all phone calls involve one-way communication, it is important we get our message across accurately once we reach our party. Seventy percent of all phone calls placed are not completed. So it is important we realize how precious our time commitment is. There are some problems connected with the phone and they are not to be minimized. But they can certainly be handled.

If your party is not in, be sure to leave a precise, clear message, and ask to have it repeated. If you find you are not receiving your messages, devise a system where all your calls are logged in a separate book, which you drop off and pick up each time you leave. Or, find someone to field calls for you. If the messages you receive are incorrect, spend some time with the message receiver, so that he or she understands how and why those messages can make the difference in bottom line profits for the company, and better service for your customers.

The person you are trying to reach may not always be available. But if you are assertive yourself, you can usually find someone else to help you. On the receiving end, it is easy to avoid troublesome calls, and they do cause interruptions, but I have found the advantages to those interruptions far outweigh any disadvantage. One advantage is that it gives you an immediate alerting of a problem. That of course, allows you to give it prompt attention and a possible quick solution. And since the biggest time robber in the United States is crisis management, I think that's important.

Take this quiz to see how you stack up against the average telephone user. Ask yourself these questions regarding your phone techniques, and see how many times you answer "yes," "no," or "sometimes."

Do you know the proper thing to say on the phone?
Do you get to the point quickly?
Do you avoid carrying on a double conversation—one on the phone, and one off?
Do you like speaking on the phone?
Do you practice remembering names?
Is it easy for you to begin a conversation?

Can you terminate a conversation gently?
Do you try to form a mental picture of the caller?
Do you keep your temper under control?
Do you avoid gossip on the phone?
Are you a professional at all times?
Do words come easily for you?
Can the other person hear your smile?
Are you easily understood?
Do you feel others are interested in what you say?
Do you keep your power or authority in check?
Do you converse on the appropriate level with each individual?
Is your voice pleasant at all times?
Do you avoid slang and red-flag words?
Are you interested in yourself and the other party?
Do you handle difficult people well?
Do you listen without interruption?
Do you use the person's name frequently?
Do you stick to the facts, without embellishing anything?
Do you avoid long conversations?

Each "yes" counts four; "sometimes" a one. If you have scored 100, perfect. If you have scored betwen 80 and 90, excellent; 70 to 79 is satisfactory, but under 70 means you need help, and you came to the right place for it.

How To Improve Telephone Skills

There are two key concepts to improving your telephone skills. One is diplomacy and the other is common sense. Ninety-nine percent of the time when you are not sure how to handle a situation, or don't know the needed information, or don't have a supervisor or manager available, using common sense and being diplomatic will take care of the situation—at least temporarily. Then, of course, as soon as possible, you should obtain the needed information and call the person in question back with it.

Remember this important point, however. Your customers do not care about company policies. And if those policies get in the way of your customers obtaining what it is they want, these policies may only serve as an irritant. Everyone thinks of his or her own problem as the most important, and if you use company policy as an excuse not to provide a solution, it does nothing to soothe feelings, even if it may in another context get you "off the hook." We all realize that there has to be company policy, but if we are to be successful we cannot treat an individual as a number, and here again this is where common sense and diplomacy are called into play. Therefore, when someone calls you, try to treat him or her as someone you are inviting into your home. Create a friendly atmosphere and hope the person will want to return. For many, *you* are the company and can make a big difference as to whether they will want to continue to be a customer.

People want you to take an interest in them. They want their strokes. Sometimes when you are dealing with people on a continuing basis, you begin to regard them as nuisances, interruptions and non-entities. You can become bored and indifferent without even realizing it. Pride and self-esteem should be an important part of your daily structure, no matter what you are doing. When you perform in the best possible manner, it is sure to reflect on everything you do. Don't settle for less than your best. Sometimes we get so involved in our own problems and day-to-day living we forget the abrasiveness and inconvenience other people experience.

Think about what they are are going through. Try to treat other people well and do the best job you can, every day. Commit to excellence. Even if you are only speaking to people on the phone, you are representing your company when you do this. Therefore, your knowledge, attitude and abilities must come through in the conversation. You may be the only person in your company this person comes in contact with on a regular basis, and since you represent your organization when you are on the telephone, you must remember what image your company is trying to create.

What is the philosophy it stands for, and just where is customer service positioned on the corporate ladder? And I am not talking about lip service, either. I mean *real* customer service. I do seminars and speeches all over the country, and no matter where I go I always ask the same question: How many people have been to Disney World or Disney Land? Invariably, 80 percent of the people in the room put their hands up. Then I ask, how many have been there twice? At least 50 percent of the 80 percent raise their hands.

Even with the high ticket prices, the long lines and waiting, people go back. Why? Because Disney spends 32 hours training all of their personnel in courtesy. Not in how to take tickets or sell soda or sweep floors, but in plain old courtesy. Yet, think about the times you contacted businesses for services you needed for yourself or your family over the telephone. How were you treated, will you go back, do they deserve to get your dollar? And ask yourself, does *your* company do this? With practice, determination and a little hard work you can develop the confidence you need to achieve excellence.

Your ability on the telephone will increase in direct proportion to your interest in the person on the other end, and your ability to deal with the information he or she needs. Be relaxed, confident and optimistic. Your voice is the only part of you anyone gets to know over the phone. It forms a lasting impression, and hopefully, it is a good one. It must be enthusiastic and must reflect happiness and a smile. People should be able to picture you in a positive manner because you presented a courteous and winnning attitude.

If you leave the line, come back quickly. There is nothing more irritating than to be put on hold. If you do take longer than expected, return to the line occasionally to assure callers you are still checking information for them. You might ask them if they prefer to wait or wish to be called back. And of course, thank them for holding.

Transfer a call only when necessary and then only after asking permission. It is a good idea to give the name, extension and department of the individual in case you are disconnected.

Hang up in a way that will leave the caller satisfied and friendly. Always put the receiver down gently and don't make anyone feel that you are impatient with them. And let them hang up first. You should hear the click in *your* ear.

Answering Calls for Others

When answering calls for others, you can follow many of the same rules, but also try to tell the caller when your co-worker is expected back or if the co-worker can be reached at another number. Be tactful in explaining a co-worker's absence and be sure to take accurate messages, including date, time, name and area code and telephone number.

Particularly important is handling calls for your boss. Again, many of the previous techniques apply, but do try to avoid the cliche, "Who's calling?" No answer to that question can be put into a "win-win" situation. Try to give a brief report, such as saying your boss is in conference or is unavailable, before asking for the identity of the person who is calling if your boss does not take all calls.

Conflict Calls

All of these rules are easy to follow when everything is going right. However, when you have someone on the other end of the line who is distraught, angry or upset, good intentions sometimes fly out the window.

It is more important at this time to use good judgment, diplomacy, tact, intelligence, and concentration than at any other time. When someone is in an emotional state, he or she does not *usually* hear what is actually said. One hears only what one wants to, and brings to the conversation many ideas that are blown out of proportion.

In order to handle these situations, you must have extremely good coping skills. How you feel about yourself, your company and the other person is very important at this point. If you are not secure within yourself and do not possess a great deal of self-esteem, you could be in for a great deal of trouble. This is the setting for abundant misinterpretations, and if we do not identify with or like our phone partner's personality, we will tend to react in a negative manner. We are also influenced by accents or dialects, regional differences, incorrect terminology and red-flag words. We must maintain our calm, or we are bringing ourselves to the angry caller's level.

71

Where do conflict calls come from? They are born, not made, usually by insensitive telephone tactics, such as: telling people they have no right to be angry, answering with a smart reply, putting them on hold, laying the blame on someone else, transferring them without permission, cutting them off, screening their calls, indifference toward them, or telling them about "company policy."

Is there any way out? Sometimes not. But these are good basic steps:

* *Compliment* the caller. Empathize. If they've been shuffled around the company before they got to you, thank them for their forbearance. A little stroking usually goes a long way.

* *Ask* enough questions so the caller really feels your interest.

* *Try* to get to the root of the problem and not be sidetracked.

* *No* matter what happens, try to act positively. If you keep a positive attitude, there CANNOT be an argument.

* *When* possible, follow a script. Your company has certain guidelines for you to follow in certain situations. If things get too complicated or difficult, call a supervisor for help.

* *Be* sure you paraphrase and echo the phrases of the caller. It will make him or her feel as though you are really listening, and clear up any misunderstandings.

* *Repeat* a caller's name as often as possible. It is imperative that you know it and pronounce it correctly. Try not to interrupt the caller if it is at all possible. Even if he or she seems to go on interminably, it gives the caller the time to vent his or her feelings and emotions.

* *Be* sure callers have YOUR name, this way they begin to feel as though they are getting personalized service. It also shows them someone is willing to take the responsiblity for their problem.

* *Use* phrases such as "how can I help?" "What would you like me to do?" "where would you like me to go from here?" Basically, offer your help. When people know you care, it makes a big difference.

* *Lower* your voice, slow down and articulate. This will soothe and calm angry callers.

* *If* they become abusive, use silence first. Then ask them to repeat what they said. Very often, that will take them back.

* *If* the situation has gone farther than you would like it to, you can say, "I feel I can no longer help you right now. Why don't we arrange to speak at another time?" No one is paid to listen to obscene or abusive language. If the silent treatment does not work, you can turn the caller over to your supervisor, or you can let the caller know in a pleasant, mild tone you will hang up if they do not stop, and then do so if they continue. If you know who they are, you can tell them you will call them back in five minutes after they have calmed down.

If, however, YOU are doing the complaining, whether it is for you or for your company, try the following:

1. Strike while the iron is hot. If there is a major problem involved, make your request while it is uppermost in everyone's mind. Don't be discouraged by poor treatment. Expect it, and deal with it effectively. If you have self-esteem, confidence and asssertiveness, you should develop a win-win situation.

2. Be organized. Before even the first attempt at negotiating, make sure you have your facts and figures in front of you.

3. If you ask for the maximum, you may get the minimum. Don't be afraid to go for broke. If you are an organized, well-spoken individual who deals with people in a positive manner, you just may get what you want.

4. When possible, approach the problem as a team. It might be possible to organize a phone campaign. There is greater force in numbers, and the situation just may lend itself to group participation.

5. Be sure you get the name of the person with whom you are speaking. How many times have you heard someone say, "I was talking with some lady in the credit department," or "I talked with three different people and they all said the same thing," but when it came time to identify those people, no one knew their names. It is very ineffective.

6. Always follow up a phone conversation with a letter that refers to the phone conversation when you want to compliment someone or when you want to register a complaint.

There are only a few don'ts to remember:

* **Do** not respond to name-calling or red-flag words. And especially, do not call people names in return.

* **Don't** transfer a caller just to get rid of him or her.
* **Don't** try to teach someone a lesson, instead solve, expedite or arbitrate the problem.
* **Don't** get bored and therefore indifferent to your responsibilities on the phone.

Look how many "do's" there are; have fun with them.

* *Help* the disoriented caller.
* *Personalize* the conversation.
* *Make* a brief apology if there is a problem and do it with a smile. Callers can always "hear" it.
* *Focus* on solutions. Make suggestions as to the steps you can take. Use the phrases: "how may I help?" and "where do we go from here?"
* *Remember* how the other person feels. Empathize instead of sympathize.
* *Draw* the other person out through active listening. Let the other person talk without interrupting him or her.
* *Ask* questions so that you keep in tune with what callers are thinking, as well as saying.
* *Speak* THEIR language, so everyone is relaxed.
* *Improve* listening by taking notes. No one will be insulted, rather they will be flattered.
* *Repeat* the customer's name as often as possible, but at LEAST three times. This is a form of stroking.
* *Have* all appropriate tools ready by the phone. This not only includes pencil and paper, but may include a phone book, certain files and research material.
* *Sound* competent and organized. It gives people a feeling of comfort and security.
* *Learn* to control the conversation with your voice. Your delivery should be dynamic and pleasant.
* *Make* a series of calls during a given time period, if possible. It is easier and more time efficient than staggering calls over a longer period.
* *Be* alert. Be able to concentrate on what is being said. Tune out distractions.
* *Check* back every 20 seconds when people are holding. They become much more patient when you do this. Be sure to ask, "May I please put you on hold?" Keep the hold to 40 seconds maximum.

CHAPTER 10
Public Speaking, Private Listening

"The best thing for being sad is to learn something."
—Merlin the Magician

People naturally suspect me of bias when I say that developing public speaking skills is essential to making it to the top. It's true, I am a public speaker by profession. But whose career would not be enhanced by the ability to speak in front of groups, on radio or television? If yours would, and you share the common fear of speaking in public, please, read on.

Here are 10 reasons to sharpen your public speaking skills. They are adapted from Margaret Bedrosian's excellent book, *Speak Like a Pro*:

1. To ensure that people listen to, remember and act on what you say.
2. To command attention and respect in meetings, business and social events.
3. To increase visibility, profits, impact and income.
4. To assess your current skills, strengths and areas that need development.
5. To rechannel stress into presentation energy.
6. To be able to take charge instantly when speaking.
7. To be able to respond appropriately to questions.
8. To strengthen and relax your voice.
9. To maintain focus under pressure.
10. To market your ideas, products and services more effectively.

The only way to become an effective public speaker is to do it—over and over again. Before I ever went into paid speaking, I had done 12,000 free speeches to promote my businesses. Prior to that, I was a communications major in college. And it still wasn't easy to get up in front of a group, have something to say and say it.

The rewards you receive from being able to communicate will far surpass any sacrifices you might have to make. If you feel you need a place to start, begin by speaking into a tape recorder. Read anything that you can into it, until you understand and are aware of what your voice can do. Then progress to a videotape recorder, and add the body language and image lessons you have already learned. Putting it all together—voice, gestures and image—will give you a total package, one which may at first seem unfamiliar.

For most people, listening to themselves or watching themselves on tape is like receiving a heart transplant—the body wants to reject this alien. That is a normal reaction, and one that you will overcome in time. A dose of humility is a healthy thing, but avoid being hyper-critical. Strive for naturalness, and remember that you are necessarily biased when it comes to self-evaluation.

Join Toastmasters. It's the best non-professional avenue for bettering speech, and it provides a peer group ready and willing to constructively criticize you. You will have to think on your feet, and learn to get your ideas across to a group who are also striving for the same skills. You will learn when humor works, and when it falls flat, when to be personal, and when to be all business. Most important, you will make your mistakes in an arena where they really don't count against you.

If you cannot join this group, by all means invest in a video camera and aim it at yourself. Practical half-inch "camcorders" are priced well below $1,000 and are easy for nearly anyone to use. Play the tapes back, and study them. Then take the acid test—speaking in front of real people.

Take every opportunity you have to get up in front of the public. As with the videotape exercise, see what is effective for you and what is not. Get feedback. As you do, you will begin to feel more comfortable in your presentations.

Make no mistake, life at the top requires public performance, and those who speak well will always be taken seriously for their power and influence.

Learning To Listen

Listening skills are also essential to success. If you don't listen, you don't learn and if you don't learn you don't grow. Face-to-face, there is no better way to convey interest than through direct eye contact. When you hold someone's attention by looking directly at them, you are assuring yourself a captive audience, at least for that moment. Eye contact assures the person that you are paying attention, and sends a message that you expect the same in return. In that way, it is a good basis for any in-person communication.

Some passive people regard direct eye contact as disconcerting, and too much certainly is. It is not polite to stare, but it is also impolite when speaking or listening to someone, to continually look away. As hard as it may be to handle, eye contact is the first, basic necessity for active listening.

The second conscious act you can make to improve communications is to separate your own personal beliefs and prejudices from whatever the other person is saying. You don't have to agree or change your viewpoint, but you do have to appreciate how your opposite number feels, and this may never be more important than when you disagree. Be objective—open your eyes to what makes someone else tick. Sometimes when we live in a cocoon we think that our way is the only way, and consciously or subconsciously may project this feeling in our communications. This may be in basic matters such as home vs. work values, or something as seemingly trivial as the weather. Understanding someone else's point of view is the second step toward good listening. Be appreciative of the feeling taking place.

Avoid selective listening. Many people hear only what they want to hear. Sometimes, this is purposeful, but often it is not. You simply become so preoccupied with your own set of priorities that there is no room for anyone else's. You cannot learn or absorb what someone's intentions are if you tune them out. You need to become observant of other people and their ideas. If you selectively listen, break it as soon as possible. As long as you shut out important parts of what you hear, you will never be able to negotiate, communicate or get to a win-win situation.

Don't Blush, Or Need To

Learn not to react to certain words that are personally distasteful. Many people use them for shock value, and while I do not advocate acceptance or use of any language you don't approve of, they are attention getters. If you tend to use words that many people would be shocked by, you should also keep this in mind: they may gain attention, but lose you respect. In the undercurrent of communication, this can create bad vibrations, which is usually not a win-win. The use of flash words is very complicated because of our emotions and personality traits. In general, avoid them. And if you hear them in a business conversation, work to not let them color your view of what is really significant in the person's message.

Good listening skills can be learned and improved, but you must first want to do this. You must practice concentrating and focusing in on a daily basis. It won't happen instantly. Even with practice, you will still tend to react instead of pro-act. Make an effort to employ some calming techniques. Stress reducers—such as deep breathing, counting to ten, thinking about something special—can help you keep your focus, and your center for effective listening.

Body language can also affect listening. Be careful that your mannerisms do not counteract feigned interest. If the smile is on your face and your eyes are meeting your partner's, you may still be giving off messages of uncertainty if you are fidgeting and changing position. Very often, these mannerisms are giving off partial "hidden agendas."

Shut Up and Listen

A good listener can produce positive results without saying a word, simply by being attentive. Haven't you solved many of your own life problems by just pouring out your heart and soul to someone? Many solutions have popped into your mind by merely having someone to talk to. You may experience a great "a-ha" as you are sorting through your thoughts. Isn't it wonderful? That is a valuable strength. You can certainly offer suggestions, but your biggest asset lies in guiding the conversation. If you offer your opinion too often, you will become a pain in the neck to someone who may be trying to formulate his. Sometimes the best advice we can give ourselves in these situations is: Shut up and listen.

Be up front if you have certain idiosyncracies, things you like or dislike, subjects you consider taboo, or topics you feel should be discussed only in certain controlled environments. Let someone know if you have an opposing viewpoint, especially if failing to do so might prove embarrassing later on.

Suppose you have stated you are unalterably opposed to hiring a certain individual because you feel he or she is unqualified. You have given all your reasons why you feel you would never be able to work with them, and somehow you find yourself working with this person on an assigned project. Sometimes our best advice goes completely unheeded. State your opinions assertively, but don't become wed to them. Don't let someone put you in a compromising position. In this situation, as in others, the tactful solution for yourself and your bosses is to be pleasantly surprised. Hopefully they will respect you for your position, and your ability to perform even when your opinion is not heeded.

Very often, silence is your biggest ally. Don't mistake it or allow others to mistake it for indifference. Silence is a very valuable tool for bringing out the other person. There is nothing wrong with being known as someone who says something only when there is something valuable to say. Don't always feel required to respond, but when a response is called for, make it without hesitation.

Techniques of Effective Listening

Use every technique you can to bring people closer to you. Lean toward them, ask questions, paraphrase what they have said so that they know you are really paying attention. Pause when you reply so they know you are considering your answer. Nod when appropriate, and add a casual remark. Anything to warm the atmosphere.

Listening studies show we now listen 65 percent of our total day. Because of all the data we receive, we can shut a lot of it out. We need to learn to pace ourselves to our speaking partner. If he or she slows down, so should we—if they speed up, we should as well. This gives us an increased awareness of the other person, and it is invaluable in getting over cultural barriers. It is true, people from New York do speak faster than people from Georgia. But more importantly, both New Yorkers and Georgians expect you to speak at their rate, and your communication will be more effective if you meet that basic expectation.

Active Listening, Passive Counseling

Beware of giving advice. It is much more effective when you are an active listener, but a passive counselor. As a counselor, you are there to guide and let the other person discover their own problems in an atmosphere of trust. Too much leading will prevent the other person from self-diagnosis and acceptance. You can play the counselor role as a friend, superior or peer, but only when it is asked for. You know you are playing a passive role when the other person is doing most of the talking.

You will be a better manager, friend and person if you listen well, and will make better decisions based on truer information. Good listening has benefits that accrue well beyond the listener.

A good listener will stimulate better speaking in another individual because of his or her attentiveness. If you can give the power of concentration to your partner, you are giving a rare gift. And it will not go unnoticed.

CHAPTER 11
How To Be an Effective Learner

"What do you want to be remembered for?" the newspaper
reporter asked a 76-year-old man.
"For never quitting."

That man's philosophy hit me in the middle of my "Be the best you can be" button, and I believe it is the basis of effective learning. To wake up every day knowing that a new experience may happen, a new contact will be made, an excitement will take over, is what life itself is all about. When you stop growing, you stop living. Effective learners have discovered that's what makes them interesting and stimulating to be around.

I also believe there is a step-by-step process to achieve this. You can add something to your life on a daily basis, regardless of the environment or atmosphere you live in, or your personality type. This chapter will show you how you can develop to become that on-top, one-step-ahead-of-everyone-else kind of person.

STEP 1: Read to Grow

First, do not ignore professional development. You can never read too many books or attend too many seminars dealing with your professional growth. If you find you don't have the time or patience to read a book from cover to cover, investigate the executive book and tape clubs that summarize the latest best-sellers on the market. They give a targeted, focused view of the material and provide you with the main point of emphasis. For those who want a more detailed picture of the research and findings of the authors, the answer might be a speed reading course. Most people who learn speed reading find it allows them to digest a far greater volume of material in less time.

Location should not be a barrier to learning. I do some of my best thinking in airline terminals. Flight delays and the flight itself provide wonderful opportunities to read books or listen to tapes on lightweight recorders. The effort is minimal and certainly more beneficial than the extra cocktail. If you hate flying, take a train. You will have even more time to learn. If you travel by car, tapes are a perfect companion, as well as being relaxing and a stress reducer. And remember, most tapes need to be repeated six times before they are absorbed and remembered.

STEP 2: Network

We have already touched on networking in a previous chapter. This is a wonderful way of developing and maintaining friendships, but what a way to learn the latest in your field! In talking with other professionals, you discover new ideas as well as test your own. Very often, you will work out problem areas simply by verbalizing them to someone else. A new person often has a totally different insight into matters that may not have occurred to you because you are so involved and close to the project. Having peers you can call on for support and guidance is an important step in learning.

Networkers can provide contacts, referrals and sources of information you might find extremely difficult to discover on your own. People are more willing to open up to someone who is a "friend of a friend." In networking, you will find you have a certain core group from which you start, but whose circle will grow as you begin to develop it. Since everything you do and experience is learning, you will soon discover the areas in which to concentrate, and the individuals who provide the greatest payoffs, in terms of leads, knowledge, content and resources. Cultivate the best, and leave the rest.

STEP 3: Bloom Where You Are

Growth on and in your present job is another phase of learning. I remember someone once asking, "Do you have twenty years of experience or one year of experience twenty times?" When you stop developing in your career path, perhaps that is when you need to start looking around for another job. You may remain with one company for several years and still continue learning, depending on your responsibilities. That is certainly worthwhile. But if you feel you are going nowhere or have plateaued, perhaps it is time to make a change. One test is to ask yourself if you no longer get excited each and every day you go to work. If not, you may be at the point where you need to reevaluate your direction. To be a winner, you need to continue to develop and if you can't do it through your current employer, you owe it to yourself to explore other possibilities.

Of course, this does not mean you cannot be effective where you are. Good performance, loyalty and constructive suggestions will be regarded by all as an indication of your ability and acumen. This goes hand-in-hand with networking, and your industry or profession is very small when it comes to recommendations and reputation. If your name continually pops up in the right circles, it is an absolute plus. Learning how and where to position yourself is an integral part of self-education.

STEP 4: Get Visibility

Whether you are coming or going, it is good to join trade associations, civic organizations and professional groups. These are the places where you are likely to meet the people who will do you some good. Usually these groups provide educational seminars which are current, issue-oriented, and fairly well-attended. Not only are you obtaining valuable information, but you are seen and respected by your peers for taking advantage of these opportunities. They also provide a common thread for discussion later on. As you get more involved, you may be called upon to chair a meeting, or serve on a panel. Your credibility certainly jumps ahead at this point.

Visibility is also important. If you attend and participate in the activities of the organization, you will almost certainly become well-known. Recognition will cause you to be asked for your opinions. Hopefully, what you say will have meaning, continuity and depth and thereby create a respect for you and your opinions. You will be talked about and referred to, thereby making you a known quantity. By being involved, you are learning. By working with others, you are learning. By preparing new material, you are learning.

When you are asked to provide a program for a group, whether civic or professional, you know you are going to be scrutinized by everyone in attendance. Whether they really do this or not is conjecture, but your personal pride should not let you approach this in any but the most serious way. Therefore, you will research, compare and analyze what you already know with new material, and synthesize it in a way that will show you know the subject or have done your best to learn it. No one who uses a professional organization properly can fail to benefit from it, both personally and professionally. And the nice thing is the benefits cut both ways.

Our society regards someone who is a leader as successful. When your name and picture begin appearing in the newspaper and trade journals, others will begin to think of you as a leader or a celebrity. The more your name and picture appears, the more successful people will consider you. The more successful you are, the more your opinion will be solicited. The more opinions you give, the more people you will meet. Exposure to more people provides more opportunities, and more opportunities has got to afford you more places and people from whom you can learn.

At the same time, the more people who recognize you and your name, the more challenges will be presented to you. Challenges provide growth, but you must remember you are only as effective as your last victory. And there is always a fresh new face, ready, willing and waiting to take your place. That is why no one can ever stop replenishing themselves. There is always room for one more star, or one more victor. To be the one, you must learn to change with the times and to be receptive to new ideas. You can only continue to teach and nurture as long as you do it well.

I mentioned "positioning" earlier. Another term for positioning is self-marketing. Can you market yourself into a certain job, office, title, peer group or organization? Most certainly. But you must lay out a plan. Your plan will require goals and timetables and may mean certain sacrifices, but it usually has rewards as well. Discovering which sacrifices are worth which rewards is another form of learning.

STEP 5: Write It Down

Try this exercise: Write down a plan on paper that lists where you want to go and how it is to be accomplished. Segment the growth patterns and the realistic deadlines. Now examine the process: Can you see a pattern of steps that provide for where you are going and where you want to be?

In this exercise, you are bound to discover that there is certain information you will need to possess to reach your targeted accomplishments. Most likely, it will take additional learning, either formal or informal, to get there. By following a step-by-step process, and keeping to a realistic timetable, you will learn the concentration and discipline you will need to reach goals which at first may seem totally unrealistic.

Equally important, you will establish a reputation as a serious and credible person, someone to be reckoned with. During the thought process, you will be re-evaluating the guidelines you are using, and refining the procedures for future use. By working it through, step-by-step, you will begin to understand where you are heading. Some of it may be distasteful (the time factor, expense, change of lifestyle) and not worth it (better you discover that now than later). Many people, and not just the young, spend four years earning a degree for a profession they "think" they will like, only to find on entering the job market, they would really rather do something else. Management "guru" Peter Drucker observes that, "Efficiency is the process of doing things right. Effectiveness is doing the right thing." By refining and retuning, you are become much more effective, because you are doing more of the right things. This results in learning.

Learning For Self-Discovery

Through the learning process you will also discover a great deal about yourself: your likes and dislikes, tolerances and intolerances, strengths and weaknesses—and, very important—just how much patience you have for the learning process. Many energetic, hard-driving people want to get to the top, and if that entails many hours of work and learning, some "go-getters" do not have the intestinal fortitude to stick it out. Some feel that if anything takes too much time, it just isn't worth it. They want results and they want them quickly. A true learner knows that things take time, and that anything worthwhile is worth waiting for. True power resides in people who can do the waiting, as long as they don't let others take advantage of them in the process.

Do your own research. It is important to learn from the past and to profit from it. One of the easiest ways to do this is to read. Read biographies of people who are currently successful or who are a part of history. See what they have done. Research and track successful companies. The business magazines are full of stories about such companies and their leadership. What is their philosophy or mission statement? What type of people do they hire? What behavior do they reward? What is their ethical and moral posture? Do they rule through participation or autonomy? Are they centralized or decentralized? Look at the answers you get and see what you can glean from them. Do you agree with their style, separate and apart from the results? Are there things you would change? Do you see the potential for even greater success?

Management philosophies of successful companies are very different from those in force only 30 years ago. Nothing is so prevalent now as change. As a consequence, those who fear change are going through tremendous stress. We have changed more in the last 30 years than we have in the previous 300. If you are not flexible and cannot adjust to the people and the world around you, you will not grow and develop. That is because you will not learn. Both your ideas and the way you do business will need to be flexible, for flexibility is the key to progression today, whether in industry or individuals. Of course, you must be stable and consistent, but that is in your performance and service. The ways you provide this performance and service can be infinitely flexible.

What do successful people and companies in the 1980s have in common? They take advantage of everything available, in transportation, communication and the demand for new products and services. Air travel has provided new opportunities for business growth and development. Computers have allowed for massive distribution of data, and people can tap into a learning network of incredible resources without ever leaving their homes, simply by plugging in a personal computer. Telecommunications allows us to sell without leaving our place of business, and to package that sales message in ways unheard of a few short years ago. We can also network with an unlimited number of new people whom we have never met. Be willing to explore the new.

What You Can't Learn in School

Many people think of learning as a formal educational process whereby you attend class, are tested, receive grades and a diploma or certificate. I will never advocate forsaking a formal education, but school is no substitute for life experience. Don't ever give up a good, highly visible and upwardly mobile form of employment to go back to school full-time. Rarely will you be able to catch up with what has happened in the meantime. There are many excellent external degree programs available today which allow you to work and go to school at the same time. Investigate them.

The classroom is an excellent place for theorizing, but you must also have a situation in which you can apply those ideas. Only then can you go back to the classroom and question the why's and wherefor's. Use the opportunities that are right in front of you. Do the work that is on your plate, and you will find, almost magically, that more will appear.

Don't spend another day without experiencing the joys of a new "a-ha." Take advantage of the knowledge of the people you come in contact with on a daily basis. Be positive and see all the possibilities. Wake up and take a step forward for the day. And never, ever go to sleep at night without being able to say, "My new thought for today is. . . ."

CHAPTER 12
How to Get Your Way, Now, and Come out Unscathed

"People who say it isn't important whether you win or lose probably lost."
—Martina Navratilova

To get your way in anything, whether it's a tennis match or a business, you have to know and understand the players. That is why it is so important to know other people's personality styles. The knowledge helps you learn how to deal with them effectively; how you prepare your dialogue, data and examples will be determined by their needs, not yours. Needs must always come first. Wants come later.

To begin to ascertain the players, you have to look at the past performance and track record of each. That way you can decide the best way to approach them and exactly what kind of payoff they may be looking for. One may want only to improve his position; another may want recognition; still another may want to feel a sense of belonging.

Winning Game Plan: Tact and Fact

If you are dealing with a board or a group of people who represent a great diversity of styles, you will need to analyze each one. Then prepare something for each, based on your assessment. You will need to chart exactly what you think the various reactions to your proposal will be, and make a realistic plan to deal with each of them. It is a good idea to write down every negative point you think they will come up with so that you answer with tact and fact.

The situation is not that different for supervisors. One of the best ways to succeed as a supervisor is to build a winning team. Part of that task includes the sometimes distasteful job of criticizing subpar performance. Everyone can take criticism, right? Wrong. And berating staff in front of others is not only insensitive, it is usually unsuccessful. International Business Machines is one Fortune 500 company that practices this doctrine with excellent results. As Buck Rodgers writes in *The IBM Way,* it is better to praise in public, and criticize in private.

"If somebody did something exceptionally well, something beyond our expectations, I made sure that as many people as possible knew about it," Rodgers explains. "I always acknowledged new ideas in front of others. This encouraged others to bring ideas to me, because they knew I wouldn't plagiarize them."

Ideas are one of the basic currencies in successful business. But no one likes to see their ideas come back with someone else's name on them. Give credit where credit is due, and the idea well will never dry up.

'Test-market' Your Ideas

When meeting with people you want to "sell" on some idea of yours, do a little test-marketing. Practice your pitch before you actually make it. This will enable you to test the waters. You will feel stronger yourself once you have researched all the various aspects of the proposal. You should also research the company and/or the individual you will be dealing with. See what their past performance has been like. How have they reacted in other situations? What is their reputation? Can you expect a fair deal? Role play the situation in front of a video camera or a peer. Then analyze or have your friend analyze what happened and how you might improve for the final "take." It is certainly a positive for you to know you can answer any "zinger" that comes your way.

I have found in my own dealings, both professional and civic, that when I have done my homework and am prepared, I usually come out on top. I also find that when I have that "difficult" person facing me, that if I give them an opportunity to vent their emotions and opinions, I usually run into far less resistance than if I try to dominate the meeting, or act as if they weren't there. If I have the answers, and can turn the question around, I notice they acquiesce quieter and quicker. I have learned this in many of the volunteer organizations where I hold a position of leadership. Since everyone is giving of their own time, they usually are not shy about expressing their opinions, and spirited debates can be held on the most trivial matters. Yet, if I do not react to any opposition that may be directed my way, and instead try to understand why they feel as strongly as they do, as I give them a chance to verbalize and be heard, their antagonism very often evaporates.

Use Free Information, And Give It

Assertive managers know how to use free information, that is, any material, facts, situations or philosophies we can discern about a person or company we have dealings with. This information may come from other people, corporate reports, or personal experience. However, the more free information we have, the more control we develop. With more control, we can be more assertive. And the more assertive we are, the better the result. Therefore, by researching each situation as much as possible, we increase our prospects for a win-win.

The key to coming out unscathed is not to show hostility during the dealings, and not to hold your adversaries' opinions against them later on. Each person is entitled to state what they think is best without fear of being punished for it later, and one form that punishment can take is overt or covert scorn, expressed at the time or later. Just as bad is grudging acceptance of another's plan. Effective leaders should certainly be able to admit when they are wrong and/or if they simply have a change of opinion. A strong person does not mind admitting a mistake. Hopefully he learns from it. And even if he is not convinced he is wrong, but will buy into something because the majority feels it is best and has decided to fly with it, this is a strong and valuable person.

Part IV: The Winning Way To The Top

Part IV. The Winning Way to Trade

CHAPTER 13
The A's, B's, C's and D's of Personality

"Everybody is talented, original and has something to say."
—Brenda Ueland

There are four basic types of personality, which we call A, B, C, and D. Most people fit into one category, although not as neatly as we would like. But there are certain tendencies that can be used to describe how any person will react to change, the challenge of a new assignment, or will play a role on a team with others. It is also helpful to understand *your* personality type when you are attempting to lead others, because no two people hear the same thing in the same way.

The Controlling A

'A' types are creative controllers. They are in constant motion. If an A is the boss, he or she will want a very capable administrative assistant. If an A *is* an assistant, look out above. He or she will want to be boss.

'A's are people who don't have to be told something twice, who like to carry the ball. They are people who make things happen, and they are exciting to be around. I like to think of 'A's as the people in the "ten items or less" line in the supermarket, who ask if they can go ahead of you because they only have one item.

They are always in a hurry, with plenty on their minds. They are "bottom-liners" who are motivated by directness and fearful of being taken advantage of.

'A's do tend to be creative, great at brainstorming. But they have one little problem. They have wonderful ideas, but when it comes to detail work, they are just not going to do it. If, however, they have an administrative assistant or secretary who can follow through, this can be the closest thing to perfection on this earth. Pushy A's come across as hostile and abrasive and cause a lot of stress when this happens.

'A'-types can also cause stress by leaving projects half-finished. Often, once the picture forms in their minds of what they will look like, to them they *have* been completed. At best, you have between 10 and 15 seconds to interest A's in something, then they will tune you out.

The Gregarious 'B'

'B's are verbal, emotional, flexible. My style is normally a 'B.' That's someone who is very outgoing, who likes to talk to people, who can't be pinned down, who doesn't like to sit behind a desk, who if they were told they had to be in an office from 9 to 5, would quit before they even began. So if you have a job for someone in your office who has to make a lot of calls and contacts, or has to go out and be visible in the community, this is the type of person you want. But if you ask that same person to come and file a report in triplicate on what their activities have been for the last two weeks, or where they have spent their expenses, or why they have been doing all of these contacting and marketing calls, they cannot do it.

They cannot make out a report. And yet you might get very upset because they are unable to document their expenses, or to say with exactitude where they have been. They may have been producing business, but you don't know who, why, what or where. It's because they can't tell you; it's not their style and you have to understand that. They are the perennial optimists who are motivated by social recognition and fearful of rejection. They love applause and the spotlight.

An off-the-wall 'B' is considered a flake, and I know this from personal experience. When my son was in first grade they sent a note home with him asking if they could thumbtack him to his seat. He was all over the class. Now he has the perfect job for a 'B.' He's a disco deejay in Madrid, Spain and he loves it.

The 'B' must be controlled because they will talk to you about anything at any time. They are the "good gossips" of the world, because they are really interested and involved. They experience the least stress because they can adjust so rapidly. Like A's, they are results-oriented.

The point is you don't ask an 'A' and 'B' to do the same thing.

The Loyal 'C'

'C' personalities are the Boy Scouts and Girl Scouts of any enterprise. They are faithful, loyal, honest and true. They are the real team players, the company person who get along with everybody. They will not rock the boat. They are wonderful as directors of personnel; they make sure everyone gets the right job. But they can't fire anyone. And they are very resistant to change, until they learn that it is in the best interest of the company. Then they are all for it. They are usually possessive and motivated by tradition. They fear the loss of stability.

You need the 'C's. They will be the great arbitrators in the office. When you have people who aren't getting along, turn them over to a 'C' and C will make sure there will be peace and harmony forevermore in your office. But don't give them too many decisions to make, because they will agonize over each one for weeks. C's just don't like to make decisions that may hurt someone. Off the wall C-types enjoy "pity parties" and frequently say "poor little me." When it gets too heavy, they finally erupt.

C's make up our support staff and comprise about 50 percent of any population, so it is extremely important to know how to deal with them. Don't try to change the price on them, sell them a new machine or get them to buy from you without referrals or testimonials.

The Detail-Oriented 'D'

'D's will not make a decision until they know all the details. You simply cannot tell a 'D' to do something until you have spelled out all the steps and the reasons for each one. Once you have done that, you can expect to get any job done to the letter. D's are great analysts, researchers and fact-finders. So if you have a task that requires plenty of documentation, give it to a D. They make the best decisions based on facts, and are motivated by logic and sequence. Their biggest fear is loss of structure and procedure. Off-the-wall D-types are the ones we call "picky, picky, picky."

D's have a high ego like the A's and B's but they express it in terms of work and performance. They take tremendous pride in what they do and question those people who jump to conclusions.

Once I was giving a seminar on this subject and a man walked up to me in the middle of it and said, "I know I'm a 'B.'" Well, just the way he said it I knew he was a 'D' and he went on to tell me that no one in the company knew what his job was and he was going to go on probation. The personnel director told me he already *was* on probation, but the man heard that news—"You're going to go on probation"—as some time in the future. Which is typical 'D.'

So I asked the personnel director what this man's job was, and I was told he was supposed to develop a training program for each of the divisions within the company. I reported this back to the man rather smartly, feeling as if I had solved a problem.

"That doesn't tell me a thing," he said. Only when it was broken down into what he was supposed to do within each division, and to repeat that process for every division, did he understand, and keep his job. To a 'D' you must spell it out.

And it is important for A's and B's to remember they are not the majority. A survey showed that more than 60 percent of people need to hear something at least six times before they understand it. You also must know by now that you cannot tell an A, B, C, and D the same thing in the same way. And if you are the person being told, you need to know that when people respond to you in a way you are not agreeable with, it may be because they have different personalities from yours. Learn it, and test it.

Take political candidates. When Walter Mondale and Ronald Reagan had their first debate, the public was asked, "Who won?" The answer: "Mondale." When asked who they would vote for, they replied "Reagan." Why? Because Mondale is up in the D-A classification, and Reagan is a true B. The press calls him the "great communicator." People like him. A similar comparison existed between Richard Nixon (A-D) and John Kennedy (B) during the Camelot era.

Jimmy Carter is a "C" all the way. A great humanitarian and champion of equal rights, but no heavy decisions in his administration. And where is Carter now that he is out of office? In his woodworking shop, working in tenements, jogging, bicycling— all typical "C" activities.

Or how about television's "talking heads"? An A-type host is Barbara Walters: in-control, to the point. Just when you think she is softening up, she zeroes in for the kill. She earns her seven-figure salary by being tough and effective.

Johnny Carson is a 'B.' No one laughs harder at Johnny than Johnny. David Brenner once said, "How can you compete with Johnny Carson? The guy's been in a good mood for 25 years." Of course that's not completely true, but that's the image he has been able to put forth, and, like Reagan and Kennedy, it has served him well.

A 'C' is Gary Collins: middle-of-the-road, charming, and extremely well-liked. But he will not rock the boat by risking anything controversial. Among talk show hosts, Dick Cavett is the most 'D': analytical, detailed, much more successful on public television than network because he doesn't have the same kind of charisma. But they all work, and show that different personalities can do the same job well, although in extremely different ways.

One positive benefit of understanding the A's, B's, C's and D's is that you will be able to combine them better. The best combinations are A's and C's and B's and D's, work-wise, even though personally they are at opposite ends. These pairs will make the best working relationships, provided they don't kill each other in the meantime.

A's and B's are assertive, while C's and D's are not. Now when B's run over you, you're going to enjoy it, because we're such wonderful people. But when A's do it, you're going to feel like you've been run over by a Mack truck.

The B's ability to be assertive means he or she can do well in a management role where their talky, touchy, feely, grabby, smiley skills can be utilized—provided there is no restriction that they come in at 9 and leave at 5. Because they are assertive enough to make things happen. The A is also assertive and will get things done, but is not usually diplomatic about it. C's and D's will work at tasks and complete them, but they are very often run over by the A's and B's.

A's and B's truly believe they were put on earth to make a difference. C's and D's follow the rules and regulations, policies and procedures. All are necessary, and all have something to contribute.

Using Assertiveness Effectively

Everyone, no matter what type they are, needs to know more about assertiveness. 'A' types who may steamroll everyone, may need to learn the difference between being assertive and aggressive. Assertiveness is merely making your point, standing up for your beliefs and moving ahead with no harm to anyone. Aggressiveness can be harmful to feelings, and can make enemies, which no one on his or her way to the top needs.

These are eleven types of assertiveness that each of us can use in dealing with people of any personality type:

1. Fogging. This is empathetic behavior—"I know how you must feel. You have a right to be angry." It can be very effective. It also buys time while you formulate a response. It is a wonderful way to calm an upset person.

2. Broken record. This is when you repeat over and over, without exasperation, what you want to say. People will eventually get the message.

3. Negative assertion. This is like a confession, admitting to whatever problem or condition you are alleged to have caused. "You're right. I did it." is very disarming.

4. Negative inquiry takes negative assertion one step further. By inquiring, "Is there anything else about me that you don't like?" you can uncover many hidden agendas. Do not use this technique unless you are prepared to hear the answers.

5. *Self-disclosure* is the 'I' statement. By putting your opinions in the first person, backed up with personal experiences, you are making it clear that this is how you feel without offending the other person. Never use a "you" statement. That is accusatory and won't produce a "win-win."

6. *Free information* is like self-disclosure, but it is more subtle. We all give and receive information about ourselves and others that we use in forming a clear picture of where the other person is coming from. Use it, where and when it is appropriate.

7. *Eye contact.* You cannot be assertive without it. Looking directly in someone's eye when you are making a point is immeasurably more effective than trying to make that same point without eye contact.

8. *Workable compromise.* When two assertive people meet on this basis, the usual result is a "win-win."

9. *Stroking.* Everyone looks for strokes, positive and negative. Hopefully, you recognize and compliment people for what they have done correctly and don't always zero in on the errors.

10. *Active listening.* Don't just be there physically, acknowledge through conversation and body language that you are really paying attention.

11. *Persistence* is the final technique. It is healthy and beneficial where no hostility is present, and who offers better examples of that than our children, who can ask for something nine, ten or as many times as it takes for us to give in?

Remember what I said at the top of this chapter. People do not neatly fit into one category. I am normally a 'B', but under pressure, I go into an 'A' mode, and take control and make things happen. I have had, on occasion, to become a 'D.' We all have to at income tax time. I had to do it when I was going for my doctorate. I hated it, but I had to do it. Sometimes in managing people, I've had to be a 'C' because I've had to get along with many different types, which is one of the things 'C's do best.

There are many other useful tools to understanding personality—both your own and others'. Having a good sense of the common differences between people, and knowing how to maximize the "win-wins" though assertive management will be invaluable in your journey to the top.

CHAPTER 14
How To Turn a 'Bad Boss' Into a Career Asset

"Few will have the greatness to bend history itself, but each of us can work to change a small portion of events. . . . It is from numberless acts of courage and belief that human history is shaped."

—Robert F. Kennedy

Success is such a small word for such a big happening. Success does not come easily. But if you can keep your eyes set on the goal you have made for yourself, and never vary, you will reach it much faster.

One of the toughest obstacles to career success is a "bad boss." These come in several types ranging from those who practice management by terrorism, to those who are such sloths that nothing of value can be gleaned from them because they have made a career out of being "missing in action." You have made a decision to work here, and, at least for the time being, with these people, so how do you accomplish that most effectively? The answer is: with great care, and an eye toward self-preservation.

Success carries with it responsibility, the responsibility to inspire others, to live up to an image, to live life to its fullest and to be the best you possibly can be. To refuse these responsibilities is to let your fellow man down. One of the most frequent violators of this trust is the "bad boss," who has managed to insulate himself from change as he practices policies that range from the inept to the sadistic.

Before we consider the bad bosses, let's look at some common characteristics of successful bosses. These are from *The Winning Performance: How America's High-Growth Midsize Companies Succeed* by Donald K. Clifford and Richard Cavanagh. The authors said America's top CEOs from a variety of businesses share the devotion to work that borders on obsession, but they note: "Individual obsession without a following is frustration . . . without perspective, it is fanatacism." They added that the winning CEOs watch certain key indicators of their businesses with intense interest and "they leave the bulk of monitoring and decision-making responsibility to the judgment of trusted lieutenants." In other words, they delegate.

This is not only because life is easier when someone else does the work, but because, even in midsize companies, the complexities of growth mean that top managers need to shift their attention from running a business to building an organization.

Clifford and Cavanagh also described characteristics of what they called "Unwinners," CEOs whose companies missed the boat. See if any of these sound familiar. Unwinners:

—Overdo the fundamental disciplines or neglect them entirely
—Overcontrol their people or abandon them entirely
—Fool themselves into believing they are stronger than they are without benefit of facts on competitors, markets and technologies
—Communicate poorly to their people, and
—Act inconsistently

If you find yourself working for someone who fits that description, beware. It is hard, as the bumper sticker says, to soar like an eagle when you work with turkeys. If the evidence is all in, it may be time to stretch your wings.

More Bad Bosses: The Hun and the People-Pleaser

Terrorist bosses are like the police, except more insidious. They don't say, "Anything you may say can be used against you," but it is. If you confide in such a person, you may be asking for trouble. The only effective approach with a boss like this is to meet fire with fire. Refuse to be bullied, or analyzed in terms of the information *you* thoughtlessly provided in a vulnerable moment. Stand up for your rights, and never look for sympathy from Attila the Hun.

At the opposite extreme is the People-Pleaser. He or she takes no risks, and therefore takes no stands. It is the approach of some vice-presidents who would like to be president. But it rarely works for them, and never for their employees, who need clear policies and someone with the guts to defend them. If you work for such a wishy-washy person, be sure to demand clarification, and make sure that you support your actions with memos that include the boss's stated position of support or at least compliance with your approach. Then when the heat comes, you will not be the only one left in the frying pan.

There are other types of bad bosses: those who believe businesses run best on internal competition, and others who abuse their power. Some call the first "managing by creative tension." In its foulest form, this is typified by decisions like asking a recently divorced couple to work next to each other, or to share a project. Other forms pit employees against each other. The solution, if you care to participate in any of these games, is to go for the win. If the competition is a real threat to your job, win the little game, cordially and by the rules. Then play your own.

It is even harder to work with an inept boss, someone who has been placed over you for reasons having less to do with skill than some other intangibles. This is the boss who does not show up, whose secretary *really* runs the department. Or he may be the character who is waiting for the ax, and so distances himself from the fray by body language and other unmistakable signals of disinterest. Your strategies in these situations vary according to the particulars. But they come down to three: Either get the kind of working relationship you need, move on, or go for the top job yourself.

If you decide on the latter approach, don't feel guilty or allow others to make you feel that way. You are only doing what you have to do. And you do not have to protect an incompetent indefinitely.

Are You Trying?

The first ingredient in getting along with anyone is that you must have a sincere liking for people. If meeting new people fills you with fear, or if you dread it when the telephone rings, you will have a definite problem adjusting to a "get along" situation. You must believe first and foremost that most people want to be liked and want to like you. One test of this belief is the fact that most people want to talk about themselves. Therefore if you ask enough questions, and the right ones, you should be on the road to making a friend.

The main way to like people—good or bad—is to like yourself first. If you don't admire your own standards or values, the job in which you work, the circumstances under which you live, and the people with whom you associate, you cannot begin to accept anyone else. You will always be too jealous, possessive or critical to let your guard down, and will always be competing. To like anyone else, you *must* like yourself first.

If you have done a self-inventory and find you are not the problem, then you have to ask: Is the boss? If he or she is, and none of the advice fits, it's time to move on. And that may be the biggest career asset that boss could have ever hoped to provide. Just be sure you have done your homework and set your goals with care. You don't want to jump from the frying pan into the fire.

CHAPTER 15
How To Jump-Start a Stalled Career

"Decide what you want most to achieve. Determine the first step toward getting what you want. Do the first thing that will move you toward what you want."
—Nido Qubein, from "Get the Best from Yourself"

OK, you've tried. You've brushed and flossed and done all your pushups and situps and said your prayers and it's still not happening. Your "career" is stuck in neutral while your dreams are in overdrive. What do you do? Well, like any good mechanic, you go back to the basics. Check for a pulse. Then see if there's any spark . . .

The basics are, of course, what do you want? Why do you want it? Do you think you deserve it? Do you have the skills or abilities necessary to get it? If not, do you know where to go to acquire those skills? Are you willing to make the changes necessary to get there? Can you still get the strength to find a pen and write down goals that mean something to you? Can you look into the future 1, 3 or 5 years to find the specific person you would like to be? Again, the question is: why not GO FOR IT!

First, you need to do some goal-setting to clarify where you want to go and the best way to go about getting there. Once that is done, look at the various opportunities available. Be realistic here. What do you know about each of the various industries, or companies within industries, that offer them? Ask yourself these adult questions:

1. Where are they? (Do you have to move?)
2. How big are they? (Is there enough upward mobility?)
3. Do they provide training? (Is there enough growth in education and learning experiences possible to justify the move?) Or,
4. Do you need additional training (language, computer skills, degrees) to qualify? Only if the answers to numbers 1, and 2 are satisfactory do you need to consider this step.

Perhaps your move is not so well-defined. If so, ask yourself these basic questions to help you define your goals. Do you want visibility and a title, or are you trying to develop an idea or a product? Are you looking for a certain income (what is it?) or is it more mental challenge that you seek? Or, to play the fish in the pond game, consider all three options: Do you want to be a big fish in a small pond? Or a small fish in a big pond? Or the biggest fish in the biggest pond? Usually, but not always, the size of the pond dictates how many can successfully swim.

Look at the industry you *are* in—and see where the direction of growth lies. Are you ready for it? Can you get in on the ground floor? What can you do to have an impact in its directions? Do you need to be a spokesman within the company or industry? Do you need to write some articles that will establish your position or credibility?

Finally, ask yourself if any or most of the fault for your plateau lies with you, and start making amends. Your other choice is to leave. And don't allow your depression over your situation to reach the point where you lose that choice.

Don't Threaten, Don't Whine

Some more definite do's and don'ts:

1. Don't threaten to move on if you are displeased with your job or working conditions. Your boss may just take you up on your offer.

2. Don't demand more salary on the basis of your knowledge that an employee you see doing comparable work is paid more. Each employee is unique, and if you are paid less, the manager probably has a reason in his mind for it. Avoid comparisons to anyone else. And don't whine.

3. Don't take it personally if your boss has simply overlooked a salary review that could make the whole situation much rosier. If possible, get a third party to inquire discreetly if you think it is an oversight rather than a subtle hint.

4. Do your best. Don't use your situation to rationalize laziness or shirk any responsibilities. If you do, it can be used to justify the poor treatment you are receiving.

5. Do make a show of your energy and concern for the job you have. Come in early (more important than staying late), and generally show how much you like your job. While your real performance may not change at all, image is everything. Make sure your image at work befits a conscientious employee on the way up.

6. Ask for advice. A subtle, but effective way of showing superiors what they need to see, namely the "new you." Don't be afraid to go into the dragon's lair and ask how you might improve your performance. If they don't have a clue, and you're still stuck, listen for the message and heed it.

Usually when we think of stalled careers, we think in terms of automobiles stuck in the road, waiting for the tow truck. But you can also stall in an airplane. It happens when the angle of your wings is too steep for the wind, and the results are even more disastrous. Aim high. Get your momentum behind you. And chase your dreams the way Snoopy goes after the Red Baron.

The stakes are high. It's your life, and your stalled career.

CHAPTER 16
Should You Go Into Business for Yourself?

"I like thinking big. I always have. To me, it's very simple. If you're going to be thinking anyway, you might as well think big."

—Donald Trump

For many of us, the desire to work for ourselves is as natural as the bird's flight from the nest. Although corporate life offers many pluses—the group health plan, company car, expense account and the structure that you can try and fit yourself into—for some it is not the way to success. But if you are willing to work even harder for yourself than you do for someone else, you can succeed as an independent entrepreneur. Here are some of other factors you should consider before you strike off on your own:

1. It's lonely out there. You may miss the influence you had when you worked for someone else, especially if it was a large, well-known company. You may feel insignificant on your own.
2. Support services are fewer. You will need to create an office, buy office supplies, and make your own coffee.
3. Money could come sporadically. This may make it more difficult to manage personal finances, and you, not some impersonal company, are liable if the business fails.
4. You will also be without the financial cushion a large corpo-

ration enjoys. You will feel more directly responsible for the success or failure of your enterprise, and that all adds up to pressure.

5. Perhaps most difficult, you will have to manage yourself. You will need to find the resources within yourself to work without a boss standing over you.

But for every negative, there is a positive. And one "pre-flight" test you might take is to see if these positives outweigh the negatives listed above:

1. You can make more money. It is true.
2. You can work your own hours, from home if you wish, without the need to consult and "sell" others before acting.
3. The size of your operation can give you flexibility to compete successfully against the "bigger fish." You can act autonomously, take risks and, if successful, reap the rewards.
4. Virtually everything you own, from your office to your car, can be deducted as a business expense. Under the new laws, you can even hire your children to work for you, and keep them out of trouble as you put money back into your business that would otherwise go to the IRS. (Of course, this assumes that your business is successful enough to be taxed. For details, consult a professional tax accountant.)
5. You can choose your work, or let it choose you. You need never be bored again.

Sound good? You bet it is. And for most entrepreneurs, 1 and 5 sound the best. The freedom from boredom, when paired with the possibility for earning what you are worth, makes a seductive combination. But look within before you leap.

For most of our careers, we are paid for how we interact with others, according to a system that is pre-determined. Ideas, while nice, are not really necessary. When you work on your own, your ideas mean the difference between success and failure. If you feel confident in your ideas, believe you really can make a better mousetrap or deliver a service better than your competition, by all means have at it. But if you are really more comfortable testing other people's ideas and products than your own, you might be better off staying in corporate life.

It is a basic choice: corporate life or independence? But to choose, you need to understand the advantages and disadvantages of each option, and how your personality fits them. Based on my own experience in both environments and interviews with men and women, I've developed three tests you can score yourself to help you decide where you belong. The first is focused on attitude, the second on self-confidence, and the third on money. I suggest you take them all before analyzing them. Answer each question honestly, and take your time.

BASIC ATTITUDE INVENTORY

Instructions: Answer by circling 1,2,,3, or 4. In each case, 1 means "absolutely true," 2 means "true most, but not all, of the time," 3 means "false most of the time," and 4 is "absolutely false."

1. A feeling of security and stability is important to me.   1   2   3   4

2. I respond well to direction; I like having a project or task defined for me, and then following through.   1   2   3   4

3. I'd rather work alone. I don't like being told what to do.   1   2   3   4

4. If I were working in sales, I'd be willing to have a ceiling on my commissions if I also had a guaranteed base income. After all, everybody has "down periods," and it'd make good sense to have a "safety net."   1   2   3   4

5. When I'm away from home, family and friends, I start missing them the first day.   1   2   3   4

6. I can get so involved in my work that I lose all track of time, even forget to eat.   1   2   3   4

7. Socializing and going to parties often bores me. I have a relatively small   1   2   3   4

circle of friends. And I often "talk
shop" in social situations.

8. Titles, credentials and official   **1**   **2**   **3**   **4**
recognition are important to me. I'd
like to see a good title under my
name on a business card.

9. I like thinking: thank God, it's   **1**   **2**   **3**   **4**
Friday, and looking forward to a
weekend off.

10. I'm a creative person. I have a lot of   **1**   **2**   **3**   **4**
original ideas. I've got a stack of
ideas for projects, inventions or
businesses I hope to work on
someday.

11. I have a lot of difficulty keeping quiet   **1**   **2**   **3**   **4**
when I see mistakes being made. I
often think of better ways to do
things.

12. I'm the person who can keep my   **1**   **2**   **3**   **4**
head when everyone around me is
losing theirs. I never panic.

Analysis

Low true scores on **1, 2, 4, 5, 8,** and **9** indicate attitudes that fit
in well in a corporate structure. The person who needs the
security of supervision and a certain paycheck, evidenced by
true answers to **1, 2** and **4,** will be prone to excessive worry,
uncertainty and stress in their own business. A true answer to **5**
and **9** indicate that you will be unwilling to sacrifice evenings,
weekends or holidays to your business when necessary—and it
will be necessary. A score of 10 or less on these questions should
point you to a corporate career.

True scores on **3, 6, 7, 10, 11,** and **12,** however, indicate the
independent, self-reliant attitudes of a successful business
owner. True answers to **3, 6,** and **10,** for example describe the
classic characteristics of the self-employed person. A true
answer to **7** indicates you are the type of person who socializes for
purposes other than for pleasure. A score for these questions of
10 or less indicates you can succeed in your own business.

SELF-CONFIDENCE INVENTORY

1. I am cautious in making decisions. I like to think things over, to "sleep on it."   1   2   3   4

2. I would rather concentrate on doing one thing well than to divide my energy and attention between many different responsibilities.   1   2   3   4

3. I believe: if there is a will, there is a way.   1   2   3   4

4. I enjoy doing things I know I do well, and gain confidence from predictable routine.   1   2   3   4

5. I believe: slow and steady wins the race.   1   2   3   4

6. I'm a persuasive person. I frequently assert my opinions in conversations, even with strangers.   1   2   3   4

7. I'm good at organizing people for a project, assigning tasks to others, and following through. I'd be a good "team captain."   1   2   3   4

8. I don't like asking for advice. If I'm lost, I'll delay stopping at a gas station for as long as possible.   1   2   3   4

9. I'm a very fast learner, and think I can learn how to run a business or a department of a business quickly.   1   2   3   4

Analysis

Low scores or "true" answers on questions **1, 2, 4, 5** and **7** are indications of a personality suited to the structured, corporate environment. A true score on question **2**, for example, indicates that you'd have great difficulty with the "wearing of many hats" common to the independent businessman. "True" on question **5** indicates your willingness to make gradual, controlled progress up the organization.

A total score for these questions of *7 or less* strongly indicates you feel comfortable and work well inside a corporate structure.

Low or true scores on the other questions, **3, 6, 8,** and **9,** indicate that you're better suited to the independence of your own business. A true anwer to question **3** is representative of the "nothing is impossible" attitude common to successful entrepreneurs. A true answer to question **9** indicates that you'd be frustrated in a corporate environment, easily bored and ready to move up before you would be able to. A score on these questions of *6 or less* indicates you'll thrive on the challenges of self-employment.

MONEY ATTITUDE INVENTORY

1. I want a lot of money. Luxury cars, expensive clothes, jewelry, travel and a first-class home are very important to me.	**1**	**2**	**3**	**4**
2. Money can't buy happiness. It's important, but there are other things more important. I believe it's possible to be a success—to be happy—without a lot of the things money has to buy.	**1**	**2**	**3**	**4**
3. I agree with this statement: Money is a good way of keeping score.	**1**	**2**	**3**	**4**
4. I want to be happy. I know a lot of people who are well-off but unhappy; but I also know people who aren't doing well financially but who are happy.	**1**	**2**	**3**	**4**
5. I'd rather invest my money in an insured, safe bank account than take a risk in something like the stock market for a higher return.	**1**	**2**	**3**	**4**
6. I mentally guess at other people's incomes, and compare them to mine.	**1**	**2**	**3**	**4**
7. I like to pick up the tab.	**1**	**2**	**3**	**4**

Analysis

Low true scores on 2, 4 and 5 indicate that you lack the money motivation characteristics of successful independent businesspeople, particularly in their early years. A true response to 5 indicates you may have difficulty with risk-taking in business.

Low true scores on **1, 3, 6,** and **7** indicate that you've got the drive to be successful and sacrifice as necessary to do so. True answers to **3** and **6** are important: most high achievers in their own businesses do believe that income level is a means of measuring a person's effectiveness and worth.

These tests can help you with the most difficult and important task anyone ever has: understanding themselves. "Know thyself," is undoubtedly the best advice ever given, but also the most difficult advice to follow. The following are a few external factors to consider before going into business for yourself.

Greener Grass, Bigger Frogs

The grass is always greener on the other side of the hill. But with our own business comes a raft of new, and not necessarily pleasant, experiences. Consider walking in to find this on Monday morning:

A. No benefits.
B. No paid vacations or holidays.
C. No structured hours.
D. No assurance of regular cash flow for the business or yourself.
E. No guarantee that your employees will stay with you.

To be successful in this hostile environment, you have to be tough. Your dedication, discipline and self-motivation must be absolute. You must be able to experience highs and even more lows, and live with your own decisions.

Need more incentives: How about your independence? How about not having to listen to any "boss" or his or her ideas about how to get it done; how about listening to your customers instead and calling your own shots? You can decide whether or when to expand, and if you have a sense of timing in addition to your on-the-job skills, you can make it pay off for you. You can be as big a frog in as big a pond as you choose. Ultimately, you decide the direction your company will take, in every respect: product, service, number of employees, etc. You can, finally, bask in the glory of your success, take a vacation when you want (providing you have done your job as an employer and have a reliable back-up). And much of what you do is deductible.

But if you can't stick to things, need lots of guidance or direction, are not a trail blazer—self-employment is not for you. On the other hand, if you like challenge, have a great deal of self-esteeem, pride and self-confidence along with good common sense and judgment—you just might make it!

Part V: Winning Converts

CHAPTER 17
How Leaders Do It

"Great necesssities call forth great leaders"
—Abigail Adams

Today, organizations (and that means the leaders of organizations) are realizing that it is impossible to have anything close to excellence if the individuals belonging to that group are not committed. To succeed, an organization must have everyone involved working their very best, and this requires more than merely applying their technical knowledge. It involves even more than "people skills." It requires a special kind of savvy, the kind leaders have.

Savvy leaders are able to get people to do what needs to be done even when they are faced with tremendous roadblocks and obstacles; to get them to work together when there is a diversity of backgrounds, cultures, economic levels and personal styles. Leaders possess a skill which is almost undefinable to not let bureaucratic infighting, politics and power struggles stop the progressive force. It takes an unusual person to know how to make things (power, regulations, people) work for them instead of against them.

Sometimes people who want to influence change purposely create unwieldy situations and relationships, so that creativity, originality and innovation will occur. If change is caused by the leader for the good of the operation, the results are usually positive. Perhaps thinking needs to be stimulated, or he/she is looking further down the road. Since people are usually apprehensive about change, hopefully these moves have been properly strategized.

If, however, the change is forced by someone else in the organization who likes to create havoc, throw a curve in a plan or generally stir things up, then the change is not likely to lead anywhere positive. These pseudo-leaders are people we put in the "difficult" category and with whom we are usually trying to cope, whether we manage them or are managed by them (see previous section). Although such people can be extremely tedious, they point out some very important problems and weaknesses. These people usually know where to focus their energies. Rather than spend time lamenting what they do, we should value them for what they uncover. We are only foolish when we don't learn from our mistakes. If we make improvements based on those suggestions, we should thank our "trouble-makers" for their help. It frustrates them no end.

The current trend is *not* to surround yourself with people like yourself. It restricts creativity and new thinking. There are no "yes" people anymore. Cooperative, willing to listen and work for the common cause—yes—but not mindless robots who "go along with the program." And the reason for this change is simple. Although "yes" men may make things easier on a day-to-day basis, they will not produce innovation. And innovation and the ability to cope with, predict, and market yourself and your business to change are keys to success in today's turbulent business world.

However, it takes strong leadership to coordinate all of these various forces. Without a leader, chaos can, and usually does result. Here are a dozen personal qualities of leaders:

1. **Persistence**
2. **Self-knowledge**
3. **Risk-taking**
4. **Accepts losses**
5. **Commitment**
6. **Consistency**
7. **Challenge**
8. **Perpetual learning**
9. **Capacity to accurately assess differences between people**

10. **Able to see interdependencies**
11. **Can identify implications of diagnosis**
12. **Able to influence large, diverse groups of people**

Persistence has been discussed in the first chapter, and in my opinion nothing will ever be more significant to your success as a leader.

Self-knowledge is also important, because you must be thoroughly aware of who and what you are before you can direct or motivate anyone else.

Risk-taking is relative. Leaders do not always feel risk is a part of their agenda—rather they tend to think it is a part of their world. Risk is something they have always lived with, and usually have done enough investigating to down-size the risks.

Leaders do not think of losses as losses. They think of them as learning experiences and challenges.

Commitment goes hand-in-hand with getting to the top.

Consistency in my mind does not necessarily relate to what you do but how you do it. Quality, conscience and ethics team up here to play a very important part of leadership.

All leaders need challenge. That's why they're leaders. Leaders do not stagnate or live in the status quo. They know you can always get better.

Perpetual learning is discussed in Chapter 11. Just remember, *if you are not learning, you are not living.*

Knowing and understanding the differences among people is what allows you to make accurate, important decisions. This creates a motivational atmosphere and climate.

The ability to *see interdependencies* is vision in its finest form. To have this ability is to be blessed with a gift.

Visualization is different from vision, and to be able to picture the results of research and action is important to the success of any project.

The ability to influence and persuade is what makes a true leader. Only when you can develop a following can you leave a legacy or issue a challenge.

Many people think leaders are born, not made and that the ability to lead people only occurs rarely, by some gift of genetic distribution. Nonsense. There is always room at the top, and anyone who wants to get there can learn the skills necessary to

WINNING WAYS

take others there. Another myth: Leadership exists *only* at the
top of an organization. Sometimes it appears this way, usually
because the person at the top is the most visible as well as the
most vocal. If a project or enterprise is successful, it is usually
the person at the top who is given the credit. We all know middle
managers who lead as effectively as any high profile CEO. In
fact, it is the aggregate leadership skills of many people which
make the head person appear to be such a fine leader. Which
brings us to our final myth: Leaders control, direct, prod and
manipulate. Some people who may appear to lead do these
things, but savvy leaders understand the nature of power: that it
increases when it is given away. You do not win any friends or
followers by using power for yourself, but rather by giving it to
others through their energies to use for the betterment of all.

Today's Leaders: The Ears Have It

Leaders in the '80s have the above qualities in common, and a
few more. They are listeners, communicators and educators.
They are judged not only by their decisions, but by their ability
to create the right atmosphere for success. A current leader
understands the perspectives of all the relevant groups, including their differences. He or she knows what power source each
group has access to, and how and when they are willing to plug
into it. This information, along with a feeling for its significance,
is the key to sensible decision-making.

Knowledge of all of the power sources allows for a visionary
agenda for action to minimize power struggles and resolve con-
flicts. A network must be created to realize that agenda. The
network should include the people, financing and product ideas
necessary to create the power sources and provide the leadership.

If you are the one pushing this agenda, bear in mind that most
educated people would rather deal with a request than a command. Pushing hurts self-esteem and professional effectiveness.
The leader must provide ways for the slow as well as the fast to
run side-by-side. The key to this is additional information. The
fast may need some of the slow (usually support staff) to buy
into the process to make something happen. Since many support

122

people do not have access to all of the facts, by sitting down and explaining them, understanding at least has a chance of being born.

Information is power. Share it with those you want to help you. At a minimum, a leader must inspire loyalty. Without that, no amount of technical proficiency can be of any long-term help in reaching your goals. Separate yourself from those people whose trust you cannot enlist. At a maximum, those you lead will share your real emotional enthusiasm and commitment to vision. Keep those people with you.

Trust Through Positioning

Warren Bennis and Burt Nanus in their excellent book *Leaders: The Strategies for Taking Charge* discuss what they call "trust through positioning." Trust, say these authors, "is the glue that maintains organizational integrity." And positioning, "is the set of actions necessary to implement the vision of the leader." It does not matter that these actions are all correct, or wise, but that they be chosen, communicated and stuck to reasonably. As the old Chinese proverb says, "If we don't change our direction, we're likely to end up where we're headed."

If you are headed for the top, you must understand what awaits you there. People are often jealous of those who have more, but they must understand and be prepared to accept the risks and accountability for what lies ahead. People love to wish for things (money, position, power) but are not always ready for the time, thought, energy, continual enthusiasm, challenges, frustrations and pressures which come with the territory. To get to the top, and stay there, you must master yourself. This will give you charisma which is invaluable in leading others.

CHAPTER 18
Counseling, Coaching and Motivating

"Management savvy is the art of inspiring new heights of achievement in people by showing them how, through example, to draw multiple value out of every action they take."
—Robert E. Levinson

Normally, when the subject of counseling employees comes up, there have been problems. There is much to say about the setting and style of these discussions, but the most important considerations are these four:

1. **Defining the real problems and not the symptoms.**
2. **Asking questions to develop further information.**
3. **Using responses that encourage further discussion in a manner that the employee understands.**
4. **Being sensitive to their clues.**

Managers must give full attention to the employee, and be prepared to wait out any silences while being equally prepared to summarize. You should think of it as a two-person interview. Start with a non-threatening topic first, then progress to the real problem, hopefully at the employee's suggestion. Employees need to organize their thoughts and prioritize their problems so that you understand them. And hopefully, if the counseling is done well, they will gain insight and have tensions reduced by dealing openly with you.

Additionally, effective counseling has these benefits:

—A better flow of information.
—Improved understanding between manager and staff.
—More time and enthusiasm in the workplace.
—Prevention of further conflict.
—Problem-solving.
—Ridding of any hidden agendas.

Often the problem that led to the counseling session is knowledge-based. To solve it, you need to know how people learn. First, as we discussed in Chapter 10, people learn by *repetition.* The average person has to hear or see the same thing six times before it is learned.

Second, learning depends on *timing.* Is it going to be told to them when they are actually going to perform that duty? In other words, if you tell them when there is no time for practice or application, they will not remember to do it that way. Timing is an important teaching tool because it's got to happen when you're going to reinforce it with an activity.

Variety is also a factor in learning. Creative people do not want to do the same things over and over and over again. That's why if you have the right kind of people who are going to be leaders, and who take initiative, you have to vary the work you give them. There are people who can be given analytical, rote jobs to do and there are others who will avoid doing them because it is not their style.

People also learn by *association.* If they know what they are doing has a relative benefit to an end result, they associate it with a whole, entire process and it makes more sense to them.

Lastly, people learn through *reinforcement,* that is, by making it very evident that their job has to happen or the whole process won't work.

BACK TO THE A, B, Cs (and Ds)

We all have a tendency to hire people like ourselves. Unfortunately, if we do that, we create an imbalance unless there are many different job assignments to do. Normally, however, we need one of each type to build an effective team. If you had four people in your office, including yourself, there should actually be one of each of these types, A,B,C, and D, which are more fully discussed in Chapter 13. Once you begin to look at people and recognize what these different characteristics are, you will understand and appreciate their personalities, and be able to combine them effectively.

You may have people in your office who are very competent, but if you have a gregarious, outgoing 'B' doing a detail-oriented 'D' job, you're not going to get the maximum out of the employee. You will not be able to motivate them, you will not be able to get them to set goals, because it is not their goal, it is *your* goal, and it is part of your style, not theirs.

The four personality types present a useful model for looking at people. Another popular method is called Transactional Analysis, popularized in the book *I'm OK, You're OK*. According to this system, each of us has three ego states: parent, adult and child. We all have them and we all function with them all day long. Parent is the tape recorder in our head, our experiences, everything that has happened to us. For example, you probably have been told all your life you have to wear clean underwear because you never know when you'll be in an accident. Well let me tell you something, it's true. I was in an accident several years ago. When I woke up on the operating table I didn't check whether I still had two arms and two legs. My first thought was as they were cutting off my dress was "I wonder if I have on clean underwear," because that was a tape that I had been indoctrinated with. Another is, "Eat everything on your plate because there are starving children in Europe."

We were all given this kind of thing. And if you say, "Gee, how come different children from different families turn out different ways?" It's because we ourselves have become different as we were bringing them up. With your first child, you practically boil the pacifier to get it back in the baby's mouth. The second child, you pick it up off the floor with dog hair and everything else and shove it back in the child's mouth because you know the child will survive. We learn, or at least we adapt.

Parent tapes are what we have processed through our minds, a product of our experiences. There are two kinds of parent. One is the *critical parent* who says "WHY did you do it that way?" And the other is the *nurturing parent* who says "I understand why you did it that way."

However, we are trying to hook the adult. The adult is non-judgmental, non-emotional, a human computer, someone like Spock on *Star Trek*, who says "the reason I want this is because it is due tomorrow and Mr. Jones will be coming in for the report and therefore I will need it by five o"clock." Simple, logical, to the point and non-judgmental. It's just stating facts. Beam me up, captain.

Then, of course, we all have the child. That's our emotional state, the person who says, "Hey, I love it!" or "Let's go to the bar" or "Gee, I did a terrific job today, let's celebrate!" That's the child. We have the "adapting child" who says "Yes, Mommy' and we have the rebellious child who says 'No, I won't do it.'

Well, the unfortunate part is that other people are also going through the parent, adult and child state at different times. I can go through all three states if I say, "Gee, I'd like to have a hot fudge sundae"—that's the child. The adult observes: "If you eat the hot fudge sundae you'll have 1,500 calories going into your body and therefore you'll gain weight." The critical parent says: "Now, Gayle, don't have that hot fudge sundae." The nurturing parent says, "I understand." And the rebellious child, hearing all this, will say, "I don't care if I'll gain weight, I *want* that sundae!"

These are all conversations we have with ourselves. Now the difference is, when you have these conversations with another party, you have to be on the same level. If I say, for example, "I would like to have the report by tomorrow at 5 o'clock. Mr. Jones will be here for it." And you say, "All right, I'll have it done by then." Or if you say, "I have other things that are due at that time; must it be done then?" we're still talking adult-to-adult.

If I say to an employee in an accusing manner, "Why didn't you get it done?"—this is a critical parent—and if you come back and say, "Well, I just didn't have time, that's why," you're responding from the child and that is what is called a cross-transaction. Remember that when most people criticize, or come from the critical parent, they have a tendency to say things in a critical fashion because they are being judgmental. And the normal internal reaction to that kind of criticism is, "Well, that's tough, I won't do it."

You have to realize that if I say, for example: "I'd like to go out for a drink after this session, how would you like that?" and you say "Gee, that sounds terrific" we're dealing child-to-child. And that's a straight and usually workable transaction.

Or if I say, "I gave that to the new girl to get out and she didn't do it." And you say, "I know. All young people are irresponsible." That's parent-to-parent, also on the same level. Although adult-to-adult is what you are usually reaching for, at least if you are dealing parent-to-parent or child-to-child, you're both on the same wavelength. When you're dealing parent-to-child or adult-to-child or adult-to-parent, you're not on the same wavelength and you're going to have problems.

Putting Personality Types into Practice

When you talk to people and you ask them to do things, you have to understand what level you and they are on. Let's say you're an A-type personality, and I have been saving every nickel and dime for three-and-a-half years to go to Mexico on Thanksgiving weekend. I go to Mexico and I come back to work Monday morning and I have had the absolutely most wonderful time I could ever want to have and you, my 'A' boss will probably say, "Gayle, do you have that report done?" You will not mention one single word about my trip to Mexico—did I have a good time, was it everything I expected? I am probably going to think of you as a very cold and unfeeling person. An 'A,' however, has completely forgotten that you ever went.

On the other hand, if the boss is a 'B' or a 'C,' he'll ask "How was your trip, did you have a good time?" The 'C' will want to know if you found any bargains, and was it worth all that waiting? The 'B' will want to know about every exciting event that went on, but the 'A' or the 'D' will not be concerned and will think it is immaterial to what is going on in the office.

You have to understand that if you are a 'B' or 'C' and are very verbal and go in and talk to a subordinate who is an 'A' or a 'D,' you will have to calm yourself down and go in more factual, more subdued and a little more in control. On the other hand, if you're an 'A' or 'D' and you come to see a 'B' or 'C' and want to ask them to do something, you'd better remark first on how the weekend was, how the kids are, did they have a good time, or did they get a chance to do their favorite activity. You cannot go in and order a 'B' or 'C' to do something, or they will resent it and react very negatively.

In a work environment, you are always trying to bring the child up to an adult level, or bring the parent down to the adult level. There are times in an office situation where there is a lot of levity, people are joking, are relaxed or perhaps a very important project has been completed and everyone is relieved, so they will respond in a childlike manner. If you come down on them too hard, you are taking the joy and pleasure out of it.

You should try to keep everything on an adult level, if it is possible. But when there is a "jump for joy," when a thing is finally done or it has clicked, usually that is from the child level, and should be appreciated as such.

Tanks, Snipers and Human Explosives

Some people are Sherman Tanks, they will roll over you. When they can't get it done, they scream and shout, and jump up and down. Their subordinates will respond—out of fear, but that's not positive.

Then there are snipers—people who wait in the wings to give you that rifle shot and call you down when you make a mistake. Those are antagonistic people, too.

Then there are the exploders, who appear to have no hostility in them at all, but they reach a certain point and then blow up. Five minutes later they very often forget what they even blew up about. Although they are not hostile people, they appear to be. Your staff needs to know there is predictability, that you'll behave fairly, that you're not out to get them, that you'll respond appropriately and that the same method of treatment is for everyone, that one person doesn't get preferred treatment for any reason. The main task of someone who tries to create and maintain a disciplined environment is predictability.

Here are some specific steps that will help your staff work more effectively:

1) State your expectations. You cannot tell someone what to do unless you give them the reasons the job needs to be done, what the results are, what you expect of them, when it's due, what it should contain and why it's necessary. You may have

thought all this out in your head, but your people don't necessarily understand. It's going on in your head, but they aren't in
there, and may not know that you have mentally solved a problem. So you have to state your expectations. Let them know
where they stand.

2) Summarize. Remember the six times rule about repetition
(otherwise I'll have to repeat it four more times). Because their
minds are on something else, they will forget what you have
said. It's important to summarize.

3) Get feedback. Ask the person to repeat what you have said.
What they have heard is not necessarily what you have told
them. They heard it based on what's going on in their mind,
based on their emotional state, based on what their experiences
are, based on their 'parent' tapes, and you know you might have
said something that was very easy—for you. If you assume
people know what you're talking about, but they do not, they
won't know how to do it. Some management courses talk about
"backward chaining," and it's done in this way. Rather than
listing steps sequentially, from 1,2,3,4, what you do is start at
the end, and work it backwards. Put all steps from the end to the
beginnning to see whether you have missed anything. Sometimes you are so familiar with the procedure, you don't see the
missing link, so start with the end result, then observe how
much time you need to get it done, charting and plotting every
step. If you don't do it this way you might very well leave out
something necessary that you assume they know.

*4. Make sure you have the employee repeat back to you what
they hear you are expecting.* Say to them, "Is this what I
understand you to say?" Many times you hear what they are
saying to you differently. This will avoid a lot of crossed communication.

Another way is to use *active listening*. Researchers tell us
that 65 percent of our lives now are spent in listening. It used to
be 45 percent. And what's happening with active listening means
you are a warm body out there reacting, in other words that you
use what we call 'echo phrases'—"uh huh, I understand, I
agree," this kind of thing—don't just sit there. Have you ever
asked someone a question, and they look at you as if they haven't
heard anything you said? Well, that is not an active listener. And
he or she is probably not a winner, either.

An active listener maintains eye contact, which is very difficult to do. It requires discipline and learning to become an active listener, but it is something you must do to be a more effective manager of people. Many times when you tell your employees something, you are talking on the phone while you are giving them an instruction and you've got your hand over the mouthpiece. You may even be writing something at the same time. Well, if you don't give them your full concentration when you're giving instructions, why do they have to give you *their* full concentration to what you're telling them? It's important for you to actively listen, and to give instructions in the proper form, too.

Coaching Is Teaching

The difference between coaching and counseling is, coaching is more about teaching. If I'm going to teach you how to keep a set of books, I'll go over what needs to be in the books, what columns to set up, what figures and items go in which columns—that is teaching.

Counseling is conferring with, having a conversation with someone, often in order to find out why the activity that you want done is not being accomplished. Note this difference. Coaching is teaching someone how to do a task. Counseling is conferring with someone to make him or her understand what the results will be if they continue to do things improperly, and to make them and yourself aware of what the problems are. And of course, in this situation, you have to check for progress. You can't think that you're going to have a counseling session with someone, and that that person will react to it and you'll never have to talk with that person again.

Counseling is a complete system, it means two or three or four sessions. You may say, "I don't have the time for it, I don't want to do it, I can't worry about whether their feelings will be hurt, I can't worry about whether they have the skills to do this, my time is too precious, I'm too harried." But if you're not going to have the time to counsel, you're not going to be an effective manager.

You must understand that everyone can be motivated, everyone has their "hot" button, and it is your job as a manager to find out what that is. For some it is money, plain and simple. For others, it is security. It might also be growth, education, benefits, location, recognition or challenge. Again, since everyone is an individual, it is difficult to keep track of what turns each person on. But the most effective coaches do it, and so can you. They know who to pat on the back, who to criticize and who to leave alone. The trick is to remember that all the different personalities you have working for you are just like that team. Your job is to get them working toward a common goal.

You must give primary consideration to setting those goals. Are they clear in your mind? Are they worth striving for? Are they dollar-driven or do they involve a greater good? Perhaps most importantly, were they determined as a team—for the betterment of the organization and everyone in it, or were they set by a single individual and passed down as a commandment to be accomplished with no questions asked, or else? Certainly we know when we are hired to do a job that there are certain obligations we need to perform. We must usually show up on time, complete assigned tasks, be courteous and conscientious, but are we motivated to go the extra distance that makes the difference between mediocrity and excellence? And how do we get there ourselves while still providing the necessary stimulating atmosphere to those around us? The answers lies in our own motivation, which is probably one of these three types:

Three Kinds of Motivation

1. Fear. This is temporary and builds a great deal of resentment. It may, however, work for months and can even work for years, but eventually the person rebels. Perhaps they quit (either mentally or physically), cause sabotage, or experience burn-out or a break-down.

2. Incentives. These are also temporary. They can be effective for short-term projects and can also stir up enthusiasm. But remember, if you have given an employee a "goodie" in the past, you must top it the next time around or there could be problems. A continuing reward program can be beneficial, providing a good standard work requirement is adhered to that requires commitment and accountability.

3. Self. The strongest of any of the three. We are our own best monitors and role models. Pride in our work and performance is the strongest report card we have. In order to be self-motivated, however, we must identify our needs, wants and priorities. These must be understood by us and communicated to others.

Most managers are not doing managers' jobs: they're doing the workers' tasks. To be an effective manager you need to get your subordinates to do the task work, the jobs that need to be done, while you are supervising, making sure everything is running smoothly. When people report to you with accomplishments, you evaluate them and then counsel them as to their next step which they then take. If you are doing all these tasks yourself, then you are not managing.

CHAPTER 19
Secrets of Negotiating: Cutting Your Losses

"When the other side sets forth their position, neither reject it nor accept it. Treat it as one possible option. Look for the interests behind it, seek out the principles which it reflects, and think about ways to improve it."
—Roger Fisher, "Getting to Yes"

The basis of all negotiation is understanding. To be an effective negotiator, you must try to understand the other person, organization or situation and help them get what they want along with doing the same for yourself. Helping people get what they want always leads to the "win-win." Many people come into a negotiation with several tricks up their sleeve. Hopefully, the reason we go into a negotiation in the first place is because we want to come to a meeting of the minds. We usually want to "make a deal" with the person or the organization he or she represents. I go in assuming it is going to result in a better situation for both parties. And I believe that if you keep these mutually agreeable outcomes—whether it's a raise, or a change in assignment, or just a clearer understanding between you and your boss—in mind, reaching agreement should not be too difficult.

Unfortunately, by the time we get to the bargaining table, we have become the recipient of so much pressure, gossip and influence, that it is often difficult to approach anything with an open mind. If we lack self-esteem and/or feel inadequate, this could also prejudice the issues. If we are dealing with someone who has power and influence, and we do not, we usually find ourselves in a weaker position, which can keep us from asserting our interest.

But none of this really has to be that way. The strong should *want* to help the weak, and the weak should learn from the strong and make this knowledge work for them.

Research Your Negotiator

Research is the key to any successful negotiation. How much do you know about the individual with whom you are negotiating? How has he or she dealt with similar issues in the past? Have they taken advantage of their customers or employees? Have they made decisions based on what is good for the company or has every decision been dollar-driven? How do others who have dealt with them feel about the way they handle themselves? The answers to these questions should help you decide whether you even want to enter into any dialogue with them. It is extremely difficult to go into a bargaining position with anyone you have negative feelings toward, because those feelings may surface in the heat of battle, and may in fact be your bottom line. If you can see yourself resigning to the fact that, "I really don't know why I expected anything different from you," you have lost before you start. You may be able to shame some attention, but don't count on it. Work through any basic hostility and need for "one upmanship" by role-playing, and try to find something about the person you can like or at least respect.

Picture yourself going into a counseling situation with a supervisor who has already expressed displeasure with your work and has issued you two warnings. OR, you are heavily over-extended financially, but in order to make it over the next six months you need an additional loan from your credit union. OR a close family member has asked to borrow your car. This person has been extremely generous in sharing their support, time and favors, in fact, they have taken care of your children three weekends in a row. BUT your car is new, and this individual, though lovely with children has difficulty with traffic regulations and has been hit with two traffic tickets in the last month.

These are just some of the ticklish situations which can and must be negotiated. I use these examples because many people think negotiations have only to do with business, politics, or important mergers. Nothing could be further from the truth. We all negotiate every day! We just don't think about it because it is a part of our daily experience. Almost everything is negotiable.

Know When You Are Negotiating, And Let Your Opponent Know

One of the main points in negotiating is to legitimize the process, that is, make it something that all parties are aware of. A good way to do this is to put it in writing. When people see a published price, they very often take it as fact. They are far less likely to argue about something they see in black and white than what is bandied about in thin air. Write it down, and if it doesn't fly, write your next offer down.

Manipulation, both subtle and overt, is often used in negotiation. For example, a technique currently taught at negotiation seminars is "I don't make the final decision." This statement always leaves an out for the person who can refer to their boss as the "final word," and of course that person is never present at the negotiation.

Other manipulative techniques include, "You'd better deal with me—because my partner is just awful when it comes to . . ." And, for most people, the known is always preferable to the unknown. Some people employ the "If you will do it just this once—then I can promise you . . ." and if it is a large company you may be afraid to tug too hard on this fish and risk letting the big one in the future go. A large order, an important introduction, a favor are all attractive bait that can be dangled in front of an inexperienced negotiator. A little nibble may be worse than the whole bite in some situations, however, and if you have to lower your price, or sell a smaller quantity on the "if-comes"— you may dig a hole you won't be able to get out of later. Judge each deal on its own merits.

Don't Rush the Process

Many people have been conditioned to expect negotiations to take time, therefore if something is settled right away, they feel cheated. For example, suppose you are are selling a car, and you decide the price should be $7,500. You thought the range should be from $5,000 to $10,000, but $7,500 seemed a nice round figure—not too high or too low. If the first person you show the car to says "OK, I'll take it!" you may be disappointed or feel you priced it too low. But if the first six people tell you they think you are out of your mind expecting that kind of money for a used car, by the time the seventh person arrrives and offers you $7,000, you are glad to take it.

Or, suppose you offer a house for sale at $75,000, the buyer bids $50,000 and you settle at $62,500. Everybody thinks they made a deal. The seller, because you were really willing to let it go at $60,000; and the buyer, because he would have gone to $65,000 if pressed. That is bargaining rather than true negotiating, but it has lessons for any negotiation, and it is the American way of doing business.

Just remember that a win needs to be for mutual satisfaction, regardless of how you reach that point. If you are going to be fighting internally, someone else will probably take over and score while you are arguing among yourselves. No one ever wants to be beaten, and they won't be if you make sure you have studied the other person's point of view.

Ethics of Negotiation: Be Honest

I have found throughout the years that honesty really is the best policy, and that if I keep the other person's feelings in mind as I enter into a dialogue with them, as well as balancing my own needs and wants, it usually helps to simplify the process. It is true that we may be as far apart on an idea as is humanly possible, but if we both have the desire to make something work, it probably will.

Explain your limitations, your authority, your needs. Put the facts on the table. If you really feel deep down that there can be no meeting of the minds—then get out. Find a game you can win. Don't spend one extra minute trying to cut the deal if you feel the other person is not being up front, or doesn't want it to happen. Don't become a toy or a pawn for someone else. But if you feel there is the slightest hope for some kind of positive settlement, then go for it.

To cut your losses, you need to be able to reach the other party—the situation and the circumstances. If you feel you are being sucked in or sucked up, then you need to stop the process. Whatever you have invested to that point, be it time or money, is nothing compared to the losses you face if you continue.

Make a decision and stick to it. Learn from your mistakes. Take mental notes on the people and circumstances involved. There is no greater teacher than experience. Use it wisely.

CHAPTER 20
Appraising Performance Without Performance Appraisals

"Excellence is nothing more than being a little bit better every day."

—Judge Lee Shapiro

Before we even talk about performance appraisals, there is one basic premise we as managers need to accept. And that is that we should have no one working for us who is not enthusiastic, dedicated, happy, responsible and competent. Tall order, you say? I don't think so. If someone does not possess all these qualities, they cannot possibly deliver customer service, nor will they be a team member.

Looked at from the other side, if I pick up a weekly paycheck for subpar performance and do not exhibit any or all of the above qualities, *why should I change?* It is ridiculous to assume that I will change just because you give me a motivational talk or provide me with more opportunity if I have always been rewarded by mediocrity. Some people like "getting by." They don't want to put out the extra effort it takes to be excellent.

And the pity is, excellence doesn't take a lot of effort. It does take a certain attitude, however. If we try to do a little bit better every day, we are at least striving for excellence. If you believe that people are a valuable commodity, and service is what every organization should provide, you are striving for excellence. If you have a positive attitude and enjoy what you do each and every day, you are striving for excellence, and you don't need a performance appraisal to tell you that.

The Roots of Self-Sabotage

Without pride and self-esteem, however, you may never reach the level of excellence you are capable of because you tend to exhibit self-defeating behavior. And that can become a vicious circle of self-sabotage. Study your patterns, and if you are a supervisor, study your employees' patterns, and take an active interest in their success. Just remember, expect the best and your people will want to be the best.

By the same token, if you do not stroke the good, positive things people do, they may figure, "Why should I try?" Praise the good at least as often as you criticize the bad. And remember to make your praise as public as possible, while keeping your criticism private.

The most effective means of working with someone who has been promoted and is not performing well in that new position is counseling. Find out what is wrong. Maybe they don't really understand how to approach people. You can say to somebody, "You're too brusque," or, "You don't know how to interrelate," or "You're going to have to make quicker decisions," but this really doesn't tell them anything. Or, and I favor this technique, you can say, "This is what's required of the job. Do you feel you can handle it?" This gets you into a meaningful, objective, two-way discussion. The least effective means is to demote. It will be bad for morale and bad for co-workers because they are losing identification with their peers, not to mention their own loss of self-esteem. Far better to transfer them laterally, if possible—not at less salary or in a lesser position, but in a different capacity, utilizing their strengths.

The Real Performance Appraisals

Performance appraisals are being given every day—by your customers, peers and co-workers, by how they talk about you, the organization and their work. Motivation and inspiration

140

start on top and work down from there. So each manager and supervisor must exhibit the energy and enthusiasm they want to see from subordinates in order for it to filter down. But each day that is allowed to pass with no input on stagnant performance is one more day to non-change which reinforces negative behavior.

As an alternative to formalized appraisals, I suggest self-evaluations. Many progressive firms utilize some form of this in their evaluations already, and they find that workers are usually harder on themselves than you would be. You will also gain great insight into your employees' feelings of self and work. Whatever form of appraisal you use, you must go over these evaluations carefully and give your input, but it is a far healthier approach.

Having people write their own job description after they are on the job awhile is another tool. No employee likes the words "and all related activities" because that phrase seems to be all-inclusive, which it is. Again, having an employee define a job is a way for you to check the employee's perception of his job and responsibilities, and done with care, can increase communication all around.

In my book, and this is my book, a manager who waits for three to six months for a "formal" performance appraisal is courting trouble. Be involved with your employees, make sure they know how you feel about their work on a daily basis, for that is the best performance appraisal there is.

Final Thoughts On Staying On Top

People—especially women—often ask me how I have done so much with my life. I believe a lot of it has been done through dedicated goal-setting. When you have definite things in mind you want to accomplish and set your course for them, something positive is going to happen.

I started with parents who were encouraging and realistic—a wonderful combination. So they instilled a lot of drive along with many expectations. I attended a college (Emerson College in Boston) where initiative was rewarded and self-confidence developed. I married a man who is supportive and secure and is not threatened by me. My husband thinks whatever I want to do is fine as long as it is my choice. My three children are independent and have cooperated fully.

Therefore, I have not had to cope with possessiveness, jealousy, or been forced to choose between loyalties. I did not have twins, triplets or quintuplets, or handicapped children, which might have made things more difficult. On the other hand, we started out with nothing but our own good health and determination. We had few material resources, no household help and no local family. So, to the extent that we made it, we made it on our own. And I believe most people can—if they set goals, persist and carry through. We are ordinary people doing ordinary things. The main difference is we do them.

The Value of Dreams

I have always liked to dream. Sometimes, the dreams were big, and sometimes small. My problem is that I don't dream a terribly long time before I want to make those dreams into a reality. And once I have that bee in my bonnet, nothing usually deters me. This has been true ever since I can remember.

My first conscious memories are of a dance recital at the age of 3. The cast in this recital each played the twelve months of the year and, as luck would have it, I was January. That meant I had to go out first and perform before any of my classmates. Talk about pressure! There I was in my beautiful skater's costume. It was satin trimmed with fur and topped off by an appropriate crown made of the same material. My mother, who was seated in the audience was far more nervous than I was, and she nearly ripped her handkerchief to shreds in her anticipation.

The music began and I went onstage. Everything went along fine until I had to do a somersault. I did it well, but in the process my crown fell off. As I bent down and put it back, the audience began to roar. I thought they were enjoying my performance, but the laughter continued, so I motioned for the piano player to stop. My mother tells me I then put my hands on my hips and would not continue until the audience calmed down. In the process I found out I had put my crown on backwards. I readjusted my headpiece, the crowd quieted and I motioned for the piano player to begin. I then finished my dance.

I mention this story only to illustrate that we all have different personality styles. Mine has always led me to be among people. I have never wanted to do the same thing over and over again, to be in the same place for a concentrated period of time or experience repitition. Yet, I value relationships, am a true and loyal friend and treat people extremely well. I have always embraced change when many people fear it. I enjoy challenges when some say I should be enjoying the steadiness of past accomplishments. I feel you should constantly strive to be better—that to me is the definition of excellence.

These personality traits are what drive us to be who we are and to accomplish what we do—all in our own way. When I was 13, I had another dream: to live in Florida. But I had a lot of things sidetracking me—family, school, expectations of others and my own dream of being a performer. Still, Florida was always on my mind. At 19, things crystallized even more and I was sure Florida and Miami in particular was where I wanted to be. I even knew what I wanted to be doing. I was going to work in a modeling school, and someday have one of my own.

With everyone yelling in my ear after college graduation about being too young, going too far away from home, being too flighty and not planning enough, I arrived in Miami. I gave myself two weeks to "make it." On the fourteenth day I got the job I wanted where I wanted, and eight months later at the age of 21, I bought the business.

I believe in dreams, and that everyone has the potential to fulfill them. But you must believe and you must commit. And you must also be willing to sacrifice, work hard and experience many disappointments along the way. Above all, when the chips are down and everyone has deserted you, you must believe in yourself, in your ideas and your commitment.